SALT and SILVER :

A Story of Hope.

JIM GREENHALF

BRADFORD LIBRARIES

Published by
Bradford Libraries
Prince's Way
BRADFORD BD1 1NN
U.K.

ISBN 0-9-07734-50-2

Typeset by Highlight Type Bureau Ltd, Bradford
Printed by Hart & Clough Ltd., Bradford

This book is dedicated to my late mother
Ellen Wade Greenhalf
who worked hard all her life to give me
a chance

TESMAN: My Goodness, Hedda! You can't think what a book that's going to be!

From Act III of Henrik Ibsen's Hedda Gabler.

Jim Greenhalf is a feature writer and columnist for Bradford's *Telegraph & Argus* newspaper. Jim, who is in his twentieth year with the T&A, won the 1990 UK Press Gazette Columnist of the Year Award and the Whitbread Feature Writer of the Year Award in 1991. In the past two years five other awards have come his way. He has published a poetic drama about the First World War *Remembrance Sunday*, which was short-listed for the 1996 Alfred Bradley Bursary, four volumes of verse, and he contributed a chapter to *Boldness Be My Friend*, a biography of the late MP, Bob Cryer, published by Bradford Libraries in 1997. His regular and hard-hitting column, Straight Talk, is hugely popular.

CONTENTS

1. MORE BALLS THAN MOST

The idea of a book about Sir Titus Salt and Jonathan Silver first suggested itself to me in April 1994. Jonathan Silver's reaction was not enthusiastic. He was interested in publicising the mill, but doubted the relevance of what he thought would be a standard biography. I had in mind something different, not quite biography, local history or chronicle, but an amalgam of all three with a dash of art, poetry, anecdote and personal reflection. Silver's edgy reluctance made explanation difficult and for several months I hesitated to raise the subject again.

And then one night in July the solution hit me like a bolt of lightning. On holiday at the time, I had spent the day re-reading my favourite plays by Chekhov and Ibsen. Twilight was gathering as I reached the passage in Hedda Gabler where the hapless Jorgen Tesman waxes lyrical, to the growing irritation of his wife, about the book which his rival, Ejlert Lövborg, has written on the theme of the future. Suddenly I put down the play and said out loud to myself, "Write the bloody book whether Silver likes it or not. Do it!" I began my researches the following day.

Many weeks were to pass before Silver grudgingly agreed to take part. He signalled this by handing me his personal Salts Mill archive, several folders thick with documents, which proved invaluable for the early chapters. My main concern was that the story of Salt and Silver should be told, and that the telling of it should be mine alone. I had no sabbatical from my job, nor the help of a researcher. I worked at nights, weekends and during holidays. Silver was never entirely happy with the decision he had made but in September 1996, Bob Duckett at Bradford Central Library expressed interest in publishing the book in time for Bradford's 1997 Centenary celebrations. I was pleased and Silver was happy.

During the course of my work I fell in love with a beautiful young woman and this experience intensified my thoughts and feelings about Salts Mill and much else. What began as an assignment, self-imposed out of inner conviction and journalistic instinct, became, literally, a labour of love. Part of this book at least is a monument to that turbulent period of my own emotional regeneration.

More Balls Than Most, the title of this introductory chapter, was once the name of a shop selling jugglers' equipment opposite Salts Mill. For me it sums up the gutsy quality common to the mill's two greatest owners: Sir Titus Salt, the 19th Century textile tycoon who built it, and Jonathan Silver, his 20th Century counterpart who rescued this amazing place from oblivion.

This book is the story of the rise, death and rebirth of a building which had housed one of the most technologically advanced industrial enterprises in the world. Now, more than 140 years later, it is the headquarters of an electronics company at the cutting edge of computer and satellite technology, and the home of the world's biggest and most varied collection of art by Bradford-born David Hockney.

It's an astonishing story of imagination and tenacity, vision and daring. Why did Salt want the mill in the first place, and what made Silver decide to buy it? Neither of them was obliged by financial circumstances to do what they did; necessity was not the driving factor.

Salt had made his millions and was looking forward to retirement when, at the age of 46, he suddenly decided to start all over again. Furthermore, once the mill was up and running Salt went on to create an entire village for his workers: 29 streets with more than 800 houses of assorted size, a school, a hospital, two places of worship, shops, a hall for recreation and adult education, and a park. He spent a fortune creating what the Practical Magazine of 1874 eulogised as a 'nation in miniature, a little kingdom within a kingdom' comparable to Egypt's great pyramids, the Hanging Gardens of Babylon and the Colossus of Rhodes'.

In 1987, Jonathan Silver was 37 and comfortably off from the sale of his clothes shops, and the sale of his fifty per cent share in the Dean Clough mills complex at Halifax. He was married with two young daughters. Yet he took the biggest gamble of his unusual life, buying a huge post-industrial property at the bottom of a hill in a run-down Victorian village more than three miles from Bradford.

Both Salt and Silver could have failed. But they succeeded, spectacularly.

Salt has his critics. They say he created a model village simply to keep his workforce docile and dependent. Such an ungenerous view assumes a perfection of human nature which Salt never claimed for himself and which his workers did not have. Salt was not without cunning - he cornered the high quality worsted market. He was also proud, as the T-shaped structure of the mill and the coat of arms he adopted both signify. However, I believe he did his mortal best to create an environment conducive to the physical and spiritual well-being of those in his employ. He cared as much as any man can for the people who worked for him. He had great moral courage, was God-fearing and compassionate. Though a hard man to shake once his mind was made up, he was given to quirky humour and displays of Byzantine extravagance when throwing parties for his workers. You won't find him included among Lytton Strachey's Eminent Victorians, however, for he shunned personal publicity and left few papers. Salt was a visionary at a time when the white heat of the Industrial Revolution was at its hottest, and the lust for money at its sharpest. I came to know about this remarkable man through Jonathan Silver.

I first met Silver in November 1987, a week after the 1853 Gallery had been opened with a champagne reception. The following extract from the subsequent article published in the Telegraph & Argus gives an idea of what that meeting was like.

Master of all he surveys: Jonathan Silver, 37, the new owner of Salts Mill in 1988.

Photo: Telegraph & Argus

Wheeling and dealing on his David Hockney treasure island at Salts Mill, black-haired, five-o-clock shadowed Jonathan Silver is behaving like a business typhoon.

He's already put in five hours at the mill when I arrived at ten in the morning, fuelling himself with mahogany-coloured tea from blue and white cups the size of soup bowls.

The piratical merchants of Smyrna (now called Izmir) by repute are shrewd, dynamic and never take no for an answer. After watching Jonathan at work for about ten minutes I reckon this 38-year-old Jewish adventurer would give the toughest Turk a run for his money.

He wants everything doing yesterday and is willing to pay extra if he can cajole, swashbuckle or argue someone into getting things done even sooner. Amid the junk-shop clutter of his orange-carpeted bridge he opens mail, answers a battery of telephones, keeps an eye on three flickering TV monitors, talks to me and issues orders to his staff.

"Oh, there's a cheque here," he says, opening an envelope. "Don't lose that. What's this? Board of Trustees...Sir Roy Strong...invite Mr & Mrs Silver, hmmmmm, that means going to London. I can't. Are you from Bradford?"

"London."

"Ah."

He's interrupted by one of the telephones. "Alan," he shouts to his colleague and friend of 25 years, Alan South. "Nigel Grizzard of Bradford Council for you." Then turning to me he says: "I've two cracked ribs at the moment because we did the work in the Gallery ourselves. It took us three weeks to do six months' work.

"Two shifts, day and night, seven days a week. In order to do it we had to sandblast 200 tons of Chelmsford 50 sand in the Gallery (10,000 sq. ft.). When we finished that we found the floor had a three-inch covering of rolled asphalt. We hired two Bobcat bulldozers to rip that off.

"Then we found the original flagstones were covered by a layer of tar, so we used sulphuric acid, hydrochloric acid, nitric acid and then 250 kilos of pearlised caustic soda to get it off."

Another phone rings. It's Peter. He's been sent to Leeds to buy tapes of classical music for the Hockney Gallery but can't locate the shop.

"Oh Peter! It's 100 yards from Argos! Go into the record shop and say Jonathan Silver has sent you to buy some records."

"How much did you pay for the mill?" I say, getting a word in edgeways.

"We've not gone public on that. I'll show you the video I did of the mill from a helicopter."

"You've got a helicopter?"

"No, I hired it for ten minutes. Cost £250. I need this film so I can see the size of the mill and what's round it." He shoves the cassette into the machine, then leafs through a grubby contacts book crammed with names and telephone numbers. "Alan, ring Marina Vaizey, Heathfield Road, London".

I say something less than flattering about Marina Vaizey's art criticism. "She might be," says Jonathan, "but she writes for The Sunday Times. Alan have you got that number?"

Alan, a quiet soul in blue denims, mumbles affirmatively.

"I can't hear you Alan, don't mumble."

Peter rings back from Leeds; there's a problem with the record shop. Jonathan snaps the phone down, picks it up and dials the number himself. "Just give me everything you've got by Erik Satie. What about Maurice Ravel's L'enfant et les Sortileges? Have you got that on compact disc? Right, we'll have to get a compact disc player today. Alan, get Dyers on the phone and tell them we want a compact disc player NOW. Don't negotiate on price. We want it now."

"Is he always like this?" I ask Alan

"Normally he's got three telephones in his hands. He's happiest with two and preferably when he's talking to someone in the room at the same time."

"Who sings that?" Jonathan is talking into a phone in his right hand. "I'll take Butterfly. What have you got by way of Barber of Seville that's good? I don't want English singers. Give me Barber of Seville by Maria Callas."

Then into the phone in his left hand he says: "Hello? This is Mr Silver. We want a compact disc player fitted today. Bring some brochures." Then into the right phone: "Right, how much does all that come to?"

The door opens and a red chair is pushed into the room by a man who looks remarkably like Colin in Eastenders. Catching sight of him. Jonathan shouts: "Robert! Get the Fish and Chip Shop." Either we're having lunch or this situation has become surreal.

"The Fish and Chip Shop," Jonathan explains, "is a very famous picture by David Hockney that's been loaned to us by a private collector."

Two men walk in. "You're A-Level Electronics aren't you?" he says

"No, we're Mercury," one of them replies.

Jonathan launches into a diatribe about his Mercury telephone system. It's not fast enough for him. He can reach America quicker than some places in England. He dials a New York number. "See, two seconds to get through." Then he dials Manchester. "Two seconds," he says. "That's how I use telephones."

The two men listen patiently. One attempts an explanation.

"Mercury is no use to me if it fouls up my dialling system," says Jonathan.

There follows an exchange about Telecom's new System X and the latest that Mercury can offer. Pointing at his bank of telephones, Jonathan says: "Take it out. We've been sold a piece of technology that's inefficient and not up to date. It's absolute rubbish. I can't use it. Take it out. I'm getting bored with this conversation, come on." And with me in his wake he sweeps out to the Hockney Gallery.

"Either you're a genius or you're mad. Which is it?"

"Well," he says smiling, "I'm not a genius. I like being a creative, romantic capitalist. My entertainment is doing things like this. I'm not into things for money. I'm motivated to make Salts successful and I define motivation as an internal need-satisfying process."

This book is an industrial biography of Salt and Silver. The mill is the link between them, uniting past and present. It is intended to be a trumpet blast of hope and inspiration, a steadfast light for those who feel the dark tunnel of the times has no end.

Salt, unquestionably the man of greater stature, represented to me, in the late 1980s and early 1990s, a symbol of enlightened concern for others at a time when social need was derided as welfare dependency. In the Sodom and Gommorah of modern life, with its greed and selfishness, it is ironic to look back in the prevailing moral darkness and see in Salt a pillar of affirming fire.

Though Silver carries a torch for his predecessor, his vision is more personal. He does not build almshouses for the poor and schools for the uneducated; he simply makes astonishing things happen. Silver is a showman, an entrepreneur, and a lover of art.

In 19th Century Britain, Bradford was the Klondyke of the industrial North; the Industrial Revolution made it what it was. Now another revolution is underway. The service sector has been unable to fill the gap left by the depletion of traditional manufacturing industry. Nor has retailing. Perhaps no single thing can revive Britain's post-industrial cities. Regeneration is the buzz word on everyone's lips; but few have any personal experience of what this really means. People look at Salts Mill today and see either the culture or the commerce. Those who do see both don't necessarily understand the relationship between the two. This is what this book seeks to explain.

The secret of Jonathan Silver's success lies in the mix. Art has attracted business and commerce which in turn have brought capital investment, jobs, new housing, as well as thousands of tourists from all over the world. Salt's palace of industry is now a palace of culture and commerce. It has even got its own police station in the former gatehouse, to help with crime prevention in the surrounding area. Perhaps the single most important word in Silver's lexicon is opportunity. An opportunity is what you make of what life offers. An opportunist, however, is merely a carpet-bagger, an exploiter of misfortune.

What Salt built and Silver brought back from the dead required not only money and luck, but faith as well. Silver, a Jewish atheist, would appear to have thrown an existential spanner in the works.

In this book I do not pretend to offer anything new to scholarship because I am not a scholar, simply a poet and a journalist eager to bring together for the first time the visions of two extraordinary men. In places I have borrowed material from disparate sources and, like a jeweller, rearranged the stones which others have mined and cut. The choice of stones, however, is entirely my own.

> Jim Greenhalf
> Bradford
> April, 1997.

2. THE BIGGEST FUNERAL IN BRADFORD

He died with the dying year, on the eve of 1877. For five days the length and breadth of the Yorkshire Ridings echoed with the news of Sir Titus Salt's passing. The legend of his charity, business acumen and God-fearing compassion spread far beyond the steep hills of industrial Bradford.

The London Times carried a death notice which must have saddened Queen Victoria, still in mourning for Prince Albert. Thirty-four years earlier she had despatched two alpaca fleeces from Windsor to Salt's Bradford mills and had been delighted with the fine, light, lustrous material into which his spinning machines and power looms had transformed them.

News of his death was carried to the farms of Lincolnshire and the warehouses of Liverpool. Among the former he had found a wife; in the latter his eye had fixed upon alpaca, that long-haired Peruvian wool other merchants had written off but which was to make Salt's fortune.

Far beyond the shores of England the news spread. To paraphrase the eulogy penned by local poet Abraham Holroyd in 1873, the name of Sir Titus Salt was known among the thickly populated nations of Europe, among the settlers in the far west of America, "In India, in China, and in the far off Australias his name is often repeated; and the manufactured goods associated with his name, are well known and appreciated."

The man who was twice baptised would have said he was doubly blessed: secure in his family, successful in his business.

Yet at school he was considered unremarkable. Steady, yes, attentive to things that concerned him, certainly; but not bright. Mr Harrison, his schoolmaster, at least had the wit to note that the quiet boy so fond of sketching was, at times, given to "random tricks". He had plenty of spirit even if he was sparing with words. Salt was not one to waste either breath or money lest he could put them to better use elsewhere.

He was rather droll despite his Charles Dickens head and Old Testament prophet's beard. He looked stern and forbidding only to those who did not know him or else had something to hide. His fancy for chequered waistcoats, his fondness for growing pineapples and bananas at home, and his strange partiality for crows, denoted a curious, Alice in Wonderland side to his nature. Would a sour faced slave-driver have invited 3,000 textile workers home to enjoy a sumptuous feast?

The man who made it all possible: a rare picture of Titus Salt (18093-1876), a pre-eminent
Victorian.
Courtesy: Bradford Libraries

But for the want of money in the family, the young Titus would have studied to become a doctor.

His 73 years constituted a long life by contemporary standards. He saw off three monarchs from the House of Hanover and survived the ministries of 18 prime ministers. He married 18-year-old Caroline Whitlam when he was 27. They were married for 46 years and had 11 children.

Political and social reform ran like railway lines through the years from 1830 to1874: the years of Whig and Liberal power. Their politics were Salt's; he grew rich on the fruit of them, principally the removal of tariff barriers and free trade.

The times were tumultuous. Salt breathed the same air as Blake, Wordsworth, William Morris, John Stuart Mill, Dickens, Gladstone, Michael Faraday, William Wilberforce and Lord Shaftesbury. Mechanical innovations, discoveries abroad, wars, upheavals at home, and the creation of stupendous works of art coloured his times and gave breath to them.

Salt was an awkward Yorkshire 11-year-old when Napoleon lost the Battle of Waterloo. In his thirtieth year Parliament abolished slavery in Britain, and in 1863 the Northern States of America followed suit.

From the Peterloo Massacre in Manchester in 1819 to the Chartists' last great stand of 1848, manufacturing England was a hotbed of unrest and agitation. Salt was in the thick of it.

In the newspaper he read with concern of Ireland's appalling famine and doubtless contemplated with misgivings the revolutions in France, the German States, Poland, Italy and Hungary. His life encompassed the fall of Metternich and the rise of Bismarck. Both the Charge of the Light Brigade and Custer's Last Stand took place during his lifetime. He saw the end of Rotten Boroughs and the introduction of the secret ballot, of which he approved.

Then, as now, Europe was in a state of consternation over the Eastern Question. Revolts against Turkish rule in Bosnia and Herzegovina had prompted bloody atrocities. The massacre of thousands of Christian Slavs by Turks required some sort of response; but politicians were divided about what to do. Germany's Chancellor, Otto von Bismarck, dismissed the suggestion of armed intervention, declaring that the rugged sheep-filled hills of the Balkans were not worth the life of one Pomeranian musketeer. On the day of Salt's funeral the Bradford Observer was worried about the likelihood of war between Russia and Turkey.

The century was not a calm sea of affluence, but a turbulent Turneresque ocean ploughed by clippers and iron steamships. Steam trains, combing machines, power looms, sewing machines, the penny post, short-hand, Morse, Braille, photography, the telephone, and ether used as an anaesthetic - all these changed the current of life, bringing new ideas, new words, possibilities and risks.

In the year of his birth Beethoven finished the Eroica Symphony. The year before his death Tolstoy's Anna Karenina was published.

The Brontës were living and writing on their hill in Haworth while Salt's five Bradford mills were pouring out worsted cloth. Cloaked and hooded, the three sisters may have hurried along the dirty paths of Bradford on Monday or Thursday - market days. Salt was 45 when Branwell, Emily and then Anne died, leaving Charlotte alone in the parsonage with her ailing and eccentric father. She may well have visited the mill after it was built, for the gold-coloured edifice was considered a wonder of the age.

Accounts of Salt's life ignore all this tumult and excitement. The usual picture is of a man whose times were parochial and whose horizons were limited. Salt was narrow only in his routine. His mind, however, was a broad canvas which stretched from Australia to Peru. Would a parochial man have even thought of buying Joseph Paxton's Crystal Palace for his works at Saltaire?

He was not a docile passenger of the times but a pioneer of a new era. That's why the news of his death spread far and wide, and why the authorities needed five days to prepare for the biggest funeral in Bradford 's history.

On a good day the drive from the family home of Crow Nest, Halifax, over the eight or nine miles to Saltaire three miles to the north of Bradford, took an hour or so. Salt's final journey on January 6th 1877 was to take much longer.

His body lay in two coffins, the inner one of lead, the outer shell of oak. Four sable Belgian horses pulled the black hearse away from the mansion shortly after nine. Snow was melting on the gravel drive; the morning was clearer and a little warmer. Five carriages carried his wife, sons, daughters and close friends. They were escorted by 16 members of the West Riding Constabulary.

As Salt departed Crow Nest for the last time, crows scavenging wintry fields or nesting in the tops of trees fluttered upwards, unnerved by the unusually heavy traffic.

Every shop along Manchester Road was closed as a mark of respect. Most mills were silent. Factory hands, mostly women, lined the way, in places five or six feet deep.

At the Horse and Trumpet hostelry the escort was joined by a contingent of Bradford Borough Police. Salt had been Bradford's Chief Constable, as well as Mayor, and for two years its Liberal Member of Parliament.

The road descended towards Bradford's vast bowl, the crucible carved out by the Ice Age, which on six days of the week boiled, smoked and stank like a witch's cauldron. The skyline was punctuated by hundreds of factory chimneys emitting neither smoke nor steam. Under the cold sky they looked like obelisks in a cemetery. Ropes cracked on flagpoles, Union Jacks rippled at half mast. Warehouses flanked the streets, rising up like the decks of ships or canyon walls.

Estimates vary, but the number of people lining the route probably exceeded 100,000. Among them may have been 14-year-old Frederick Delius whose father Julius, a wool merchant, would certainly have been acquainted with Salt or his son Titus junior. Delius, his mind on music even then, was six years away from leaving Bradford for Florida.

The funeral was a spectacle to behold; not to have watched it pass would have been thought perverse. Each person standing in the mucky, churned-up footpaths perhaps sensed that he or she was witnessing the passing of history. The crowd was reportedly in subdued mood, nevertheless the route into town was lined by policemen.

Bradford, 20 years away from city status, was in the throes of transforming itself from the filthiest hole in the country to a place of grandeur.

Focal point and chief symbol of its pride was the new Town Hall, its pale gold sandstone like the freshly-shaved face of an alderman on his first civic day. In the central Tuscan tower the huge bell tolled. The exterior sculpture gallery of England's monarchs, each one recessed on its own stone pedestal, gazed down at the VIPs filling the town hall square. Such a congregation of notables the town had never seen - not even when Lord Palmerston laid the foundation stone of the Wool Exchange and Charles Dickens - the 'Boz' who had satirised Salt's discovery of alpaca - gave a reading at St George's Hall.

The great and the good were shepherded to their allotted places before the Town Hall steps by policemen holding up numbered placards.

There were MPs, peers of the realm, eminent clergymen, members of Bradford Town Council, borough and county magistrates, representatives of the Chamber of Commerce and about 100 from the Liberal Club. They came from Bradford Grammar School, the Infirmary, Bradford Mechanics' Institute, the Board of Hope Union, Bradford Nurses' Training Institution, the Sailors' Orphanage in Hull, the Yorkshire College of Science, the Royal Albert Asylum in Lancaster. The throng included about 90 members of the Independent Order of Oddfellows, representatives from the Licensed Victuallers' Association (ironic bearing in mind Salt's views of the bad influence of public houses on working people), the Conservative Association, as well as numerous charities to which Salt has distributed many thousands of pounds.

The arrival of the cortege was the signal for this vast concourse of uniforms, black suits, sable frocks and crepe hats to start the journey to Saltaire.

Seventy carriages carrying 13 chief mourners and 65 mourners churned up the rutted road. The respective bands of the 2nd West Yorkshire Artillery Volunteers and 3rd West Yorkshire Rifle Volunteers played the Dead March as the bells of both the Town Hall and the parish church boomed.

The procession passed the seated marble statue of Sir Titus by J. Adams-Acton, for which the people of Bradford had raised the money. Placed in front of the Town Hall in 1874, it was removed a mere 20 years after Salt's death and carted down Manningham Lane to an obscure corner of Lister Park. Thereafter Salt, alone on his pedestal, was left to erode, gazing forlornly in the direction of his beloved Saltaire. That morning, however, the black wrought iron railings round the statue were festooned with evergreens; the statue itself was draped with black cloth.

Thirty minutes after the head of the procession had started to move, the rear of the column left the square.

Business had been suspended for the morning in Lockwood and Mawson's Wool

Exchange, the Italianate building which the mighty John Ruskin had pooh-poohed. Hatless woolmen stood at every window.

Directly opposite, the columns and arches of Swan Arcade were rising from builders' scaffolding. Its corridors would one day echo with the footsteps of a young and flamboyantly dressed J.B. Priestley, hurrying from his clerk's office to Lyons Tea and Coffee House or the Talbot Hotel, where Branwell Brontë had once done his drinking. Later the building would be the object of the open-faced admiration of a young Bradford art student wheeling his home-made cart of paints and brushes about the city. David Hockney was to say that Swan Arcade was as good as anything in Paris. That, however, did not come into the reckoning of Stanley Wardley, Bradford's former chief engineer who crassly ordered its demolition 90-odd years after Salt's funeral.

Out of Market Street, left into Cheapside, and then the gradient up to Manningham Lane with its ornate gas lamps and trees. Salt's first family home had been here. Manningham Lane, cut into the side of a hill below which ran Bradford's first railway, was the main artery into the blue-blooded part of town. Large houses and villas were set back from the dirt and dust of the road. One such suburban arcadia was Clifton Villas. The architects William Mawson and his brother Richard lived at number 2. Eighty years after Salt's death, Jonathan Silver was growing up at 4 Clifton Villas.

These days Manningham Lane, with its unbecoming jumble of old and modern facades, its flagstoned pavements replaced by characterless bitumen, its once gracious homes converted into offices or take-aways, resembles downtown Los Angeles. Bradford's post-industrial decline, its loss of self respect and confidence in the future, can be measured in the slump from elegance to decadence of this once-dignified and handsome thoroughfare. On the second night of rioting by Muslim youths in June 1995, more than 100 businesses were attacked and 66 cars burned. Many plate-glass windows were cracked or smashed. Some remained boarded up for weeks afterwards. Central Bradford looked as though it was being crated up for removal.

Salt's funeral procession reached back for three-quarters of a mile. It was joined at the bottom end of Lister Park by 320 people from Shipley and Saltaire. As they clambered over the banked-up slush shovelled out of the road by specially employed scavengers, the commotion alarmed one of the horses which bolted, scattering spectators in the coconut ice of snow and mud. The frightened animal was caught and pacified at Frizinghall.

More than four hours had passed since the cortege had disturbed the crows at Halifax. Now more than a mile long, it started the descent along unmade-up roads to Saltaire.

The day was proving to be a long one for the 160 constables, 11 sergeants, three inspectors and two superintendents on duty. That afternoon they were to receive the civic thanks of Bradford's Mayor, George Motley Waud.

The Bradford Observer's anonymous correspondents - reporters did not get by-lines in those days - took the temperature of the crowd's mood. "The general feeling seemed to be one which is natural on such occasions when a great loss is fresh on the

This magnificent watercolour of Titus Salt by artist Simon Palmer depicts Salt's Alice in Wonderland quality. Note the enlarged watch.

Courtesy: Simon Palmer & Jonathan Silver

mind - that such a loss could never be sustained again," they reported in the following day's paper.

However, some present seemed not to regret the old man's passing. They remembered the strikes of 1868 and 1876 - the latter had gone on for two weeks. Salt had got his way as usual. For all his good works he was still a boss, one of 'them', a rich man who ruled the resentments of others. But for the majority of those lining Victoria Road, blinds closed in all the houses, Salt was "as complete an example of Christian manliness" whose like they would not see again.

Salt's chapel stands across the road from the mill. The siting of each building, the relation of one to the other, is pithily summed up by Jack Reynolds in his book The Great Paternalist.

"Church and factory stood closely juxtaposed on opposite sides of the road, for the business of God was the business of the world and the business of the world was the business of God." Twelve foremen from the works carried the double-coffin on a wooden frame prepared for the occasion. More than 400 people who had worked for Salt for just under 20 years congregated in the chapel's grounds; another 70 or so who had remained in his employ for 20 to 40 years waited inside.

John Firth, the organist, played Mendlesohn's Funeral March in A Minor and appropriately, part of Beethoven's Eroica. The service began at 1.30pm. Afterwards, thousands filed past the coffin which remained on its wooden catafalque outside the family mausoleum until the following day. So great was the number of people who wished to say goodbye that the mausoleum was kept unsealed for a week.

Later that day, perhaps by the light of a flickering candle, Abraham Holroyd, sat down in his Saltaire house and wrote a five-verse lament in memory of the man whose profile he had written in 1873. The final verse is as follows:-

> Toll the bell! Then toll the bell!
> Toll the good man's funeral knell.
> Beat the solemn muffled drum,
> Let the moaning music come:
> Thousands mourn the loss to-day,
> Of a good man passed away;
> And words will fail to tell his worth
> Who has seen the last of earth.

The following Sunday, funeral sermons were preached in Salt's memory in many churches. At Lightcliffe, the Rev. J. Thompson summed up the founder of Salts Mill and the Saltaire village.

"The rising from one position to another in the social scale, had no effect on his friendships. The friends of his youth were with him to the close; or, if not, it was they who had fallen asleep, or fallen away from him, and those noble enterprises to which he had consecrated his strength and resources. He was a pioneer; a creator of the new era."

3. HEROIC MATERIALISM

Unlike the political revolutions which reshaped France from 1789, Russia from 1917 and Germany from 1933, the Industrial Revolution had no programme; nor was it carried forward by activists with a definite vision and sense of national destiny.

The Industrial Revolution is simply the generic name given to a set of changing circumstances, inventions and discoveries, starting somewhere in the late 18th Century. It was not a mighty rushing river so much as a series of tributaries. The flood of manufacturing, when it came, was not a national phenomenon presided over by a central committee with a five year plan.

In his book The Birth of Europe, Michael Andrews says Britain's Industrial Revolution was essentially regional, developing on a small scale with limited amounts of capital in widely separated parts of the country - long before the country was bound together by the wire and steel of the electric telegraph and the railways. Local wealth encouraged regional independence.

"This was reflected in the rapid rise of Manchester - which looked for its interests not to London and Europe but across the Atlantic," Andrews says. In fact, to the cotton plantations of the southern states of pre-Civil War America. "Self-sufficiency and internationalism gave the region an exposure to independent thought and ideas which were able to take root in a new, increasingly wealthy middle-class."

The greatest happiness of the greatest number espoused by Jeremy Bentham really only applied to comparatively few. The disenfranchised majority were there merely to stoke the boilers of the Industrial Revolution.

The rise of middle-class affluence was not confined to Britain, as the following observation from the Age of Optimism, in the Newsweek book Milestones of History, shows.

"In some parts of Europe an almost morbid cupidity was elevated into a cult of money for its own sake, a philosophy that frequently went side by side with harebrained schemes of rash investment. The extremes that such cupidity reached in France were satirised in the novels of Honore de Balzac."

Manufacturing wealth of the middle-class brought with it desires, especially the desire for empowerment. The newly-rich of Liverpool, Birmingham and Manchester were neither gentlemen nor aristocrats; class was still based on birth, and wealth was measured in acres rather than yards of cloth. This new breed of self-made men had

The worsted capital of the world c1870 proving that muck and brass are not incompatible.

Courtesy: Bradford Libraries

nothing in common with the likes of Lord Liverpool and Lord Castlereagh. The class of landed aristocracy and high churchmen must have watched with a mixture of apprehension and incredulity as this new class, with its demands for political reform and social change, loomed ever larger on England's green and enclosed pleasant land.

"The new discoveries which created the Industrial Revolution (in the late 18th Century) were made by men outside the Royal Society and the universities. They were found in the manufacturing towns, and in the academies of the dissenters, to which manufacturers sent their sons because they gave a more realistic education than the universities," write Jacob Bronowski and Bruce Mazlisch in The Western Intellectual Tradition.

Joseph Priestley, the chemist whose discovery of oxygen destroyed the widely-held belief that air was one of four elements, was born in Birstall, Yorkshire, in 1733, and studied at the Warrington Academy, Lancashire. Manchester had its Philosophical Society (Richard Cobden, John Bright and Robert Owen were members), as did Leeds; and Birmingham had its Lunar Society.

"The most active mind in the Lunar Society was Matthew Boulton, James Watt's partner in the making of steam engines," say Bronowski and Mazlisch. This new generation of practical men "did not see the world as a dying classical tragedy". They saw it as a place of opportunities; they believed strongly in their right to shape and forge their own individual destiny. Unlike the aristocracy, whose education began and ended with Greek palaces and Roman temples, this new generation was not obsessed with the past, at least not the classical past with its fluted columns and amputated statues.

The new cathedrals of the Industrial Revolution were railway stations. They were built of iron and steel. Public buildings were handsome stone and brick monuments. In Bradford the architecture that was to be the permanent symbol of this new class was inspired by Christian Renaissance Italy. Regionalism embraced the world, and in due course a good part of the world flocked to the regions of northern industrial England, to towns like Bradford.

Irish labourers built railways and viaducts; later famine drove whole families from Ireland into English wool towns to seek their bread. Jews and Germans constructed vast warehouses and traded on world markets. Regionalism begat cosmopolitanism, a willingness to look abroad for new ideas and materials.

Titus Salt is one of the most remarkable examples of this development.

In many ways dyed-in-the-wool and old fashioned (he did not go in for novels and poetry), this most regional of Yorkshire men made his fortune by spinning and weaving wool from southern Russia and the mountains of Peru. When he built (but not for himself), he did so on a scale and in a style which embodied aesthetic grandeur and a sense of destiny. His buildings were made to last. They were symbols of the age which he, who had inherited nothing, helped to create.

"Bradford has never merely dealt with this place and that, but has dealt with the whole world, putting a best coat and waistcoat on the planet itself," wrote J.B.

Priestley. He knew what he was talking about.

The Bradford into which he was born in 1894 had earned its reputation as Wool Capital of the World, trading from Australia to Peru. To paraphrase an old poem, Bradford was Peru.

This had yet to happen when Titus Salt was born to Grace and Daniel Salt in Morley in 1803. That was the year John Rand built Bradford's first spinning mill, one year after the first factory act banned workhouse children from labouring for more than 11 hours a day in textile mills.

There is a print of Bradford in 1718-19 which shows little more than a collection of houses and a parish church. By 1803 coal and iron-ore were being mined, but to no large degree: Bradford looked much the same as it had to the artist who had made that drawing. Its hills were still green and cloudy.

Only four stage-coaches rattled in and out of the place - it wasn't even a town - by the end of the Napoleonic Wars. Yet by 1825 the number of coaches had increased to 28. The manufacture of woollen products was the staple industry.

In 1822 there were only five worsted mills. By 1861 Bradford, by then a town, had 157.

When Titus Salt was born Bradford's population was less than 14,000. A mere 47 years later in 1850, well over 100,000 people lived among its mills and dye houses, warehouses and taverns. Bradford had grown faster than Birmingham, Leeds, Liverpool, Manchester and Bristol.

Jack Reynolds states that by the middle of the century the parish of Bradford had almost half the productive capacity of Britain's worsted trade.

Manchester, where Jonathan Silver was to open his first clothes shop, is usually thought of as the powerhouse of the Industrial Revolution, importing vast quantities of cotton and transforming it into finished products for the rest of the world. But Bradford was a veritable Klondyke of the golden age of manufacture.

In carving out Bradford's Pennine basin, the Ice Age had left rich deposits in the rocks and soil which the age of steam and railways would rapaciously exploit to the full. There was no gold in 'them thar hills', but raw materials just as priceless: soft water in abundance, ideal for rinsing and cleansing greasy wool; coal; iron-ore; and wondrous gold-coloured sandstone.

By 1868 there were 56 collieries in Bradford and Bingley, producing nearly 1.9 million tons of coal out of 9.7 million tons for the whole of the three Yorkshire Ridings. The same year the West Riding produced 785,628 tons of iron ore of which nearly 600,000 tons came from the Low Moor area of Bradford.

"Steam power was Bradford's life: a canal its first necessity: the railway its access to the world," writes Malcolm Hardman in his book Ruskin and Bradford: An Experiment in Victorian Cultural History.

"The (Leeds-Liverpool) canal of 1774 made it possible to get at the limestone of the Upper Aire Valley, essential to the iron industry. The Bowling Iron Works were constructed and for a time gained almost a monopoly in the production of armaments of truly pulverising quality. Low Moor Iron Works were constructed; and took the lead in railway and marine engineering. They provided part of the Atlantic telegraph cable of 1858-66.

"The world's largest output of wool combing, in velvet manufacture, in alpaca, in piece-dyeing of cloth of all kinds - raw materials for these examples of Bradford work had to be brought from South America, from Australia, from the continent of Europe, and to be sent back again at a profit. India and China and Russia must be open to Bradford too.

"If Bradford was to make textile goods for the world, the world's communication system must be shaped and its wars influenced by Bradford's iron goods."   What did that Old Testament-bearded poet of commodities and author of The Communist Manifesto, Karl Marx, have to say about the new class of manufacturers and the industrial age they had created in their own image?

"The bourgeoisie, during its rule of scarce one hundred years, has created more massive and more colossal productive forces than all preceding generations together. Subjection of Nature's forces to man, machinery, application of chemistry to industry and agriculture, steam navigation, railways, electric telegraphs, clearing of whole continents for cultivation, canalisation of rivers, whole populations conjured out of the ground - what earlier century had even a presentiment that such productive forces slumbered in the lap of social labour."

Titus Salt's connection with Bradford began at about the age of 20. The transition from rural Pennine's backwater to industrial Hercules occurred exactly during Salt's rise to maturity and wealth. As Jack Reynolds observes, his career covers the years of Bradford's greatest urban and economic expansion and "reads like a comment on the Victorian idea of progress."   Salt played a central role in bringing about what art historian Kenneth Clark was to describe as the age of "heroic materialism".

4. THE GOLDEN FLEECE

Anyone with a new idea at the start of an industrial trend, or an era of technological innovation, is likely to be successful. Pace Micro Technology, the rapidly expanding electronics company now based in Salts Mill, is a modern example of this principle.

Pace started off as a one-man concern in a Bradford back-bedroom in the mid-1980s, a period of devastation for traditional manufacturing. Making equipment for satellite dishes was better suited to the times. The Government was about to deregulate broadcasting, opening up the airwaves to small production companies and new conglomerates.

Pace boomed. In 1994 the company won a £20 million order to supply decoders, satellite receiver/decoders and cable receivers to the Far East. The following year Pace won export contracts to Asia and Australia worth £300 million. In 1996 half the company was floated on the stock market with a valuation of nearly half a billion pounds.

Robert Fleming, Pace's operations director, said: "If Titus Salt were alive today I think it's possible he would be doing what we are doing. It's exciting and makes money. I doubt if he would be in the wool industry, or the car industry, or the coal industry," I doubt if there is much of a coal industry, indigenous car industry or wool industry left in the United Kingdom in which a man like Titus Salt could flourish.

The 19th Century equivalents of Pace's decoders and receivers were cotton and wool textiles. They were sold throughout the world. In the 1760s English cotton exports were worth an average of £200,000 a year. By 1829 their value exceeded £37 million.

In 1824, when the strapping 21-year-old Titus Salt was learning his trade at the Bradford wool stapling firm of Messrs Rouse and Son, the British Government removed the barrier to wool exports. This had been maintained for hundreds of years because we were scared the rest of the world would learn how to mass produce wool textiles and beat us at our own game. The liberalisation of corn was to follow in the 1840s.

By the time Titus Salt had learned to identify the ten different qualities of a fleece, wool textiles were thriving. The West Riding, with its abundance of raw material and skilled labour, was ideally placed to take full advantage of the technological changes which had created the new affluence.

Edward Baines, writing in the 1870s, listed four principal factors in the West

Salt spun and wove the hair of the alpaca Llama from Peru into a lustrous light material. *Courtesy: Simon Palmer & Jonathan Silver*

Riding's favour: the greater cheapness of coal and iron; a large body of men capable of making and operating machinery; access to the eastern and western ports of Hull and Liverpool; and a plentiful supply of soft water suitable for washing raw wool.

Salt was in the right place at the right time; just as importantly, he was in the right business.

'Textiles' is a blanket term which may mean little to anyone with no personal or family experience of this type of manufacturing. Traipsing round an industrial museum full of inactive lumps of spinning and weaving machinery is unlikely to bring the subject to life unless you know a little about the materials for which they were designed, and the different functions they performed.

Colum Giles and Ian H. Goodall, in their book Yorkshire Textile Mills 1770-1930, explain. "The Yorkshire textile industry used four principal raw materials: two animal fibres (wool and silk) and two vegetable fibres (cotton and flax). In addition hair (mohair, alpaca, angora, vicuna) was used in the wool sector.

"The wool sector was divided into three branches according to the material processed: short-staple wool was used for woollens, long-staple wool for worsted, and wool waste material (known as shoddy) in the recovered wool branch.

"As long-stapled fibres, mohair and alpaca were treated as worsted wools and therefore belonged to the worsted branch. To a large extent, most Yorkshire mills dealt exclusively with one type of material."

Different processes were used. Wool intended for woollen goods had a short staple or grain and was prepared for spinning by carding. 'Felting', the bonding together of the fibres, was important for the production of woollen goods. Longer staple wool for worsteds was combed out with hot implements. The felting property was not required for worsted stuffs.

Worsted took off for two main reasons: firstly, improvements in the process of mechanised combing made old practices redundant; secondly, cotton warps were introduced which cheapened the raw material of worsted manufacture.

In 1857, four years after the completion of Salt's state-of-the-art worsted mill, almost twice the number of people worked in worsted mills than in woollen mills - approximately 79,000 as against 43,000. Four-fifths of those engaged in worsted manufacture worked in mills, whereas many of those in the woollen business, hand loom weavers for instance, worked at home or in smaller units called shops.

Worsted, otherwise known as mixed-fibre cloths, played a key role in Yorkshire's textile industry, as Colum Giles and Ian Goodall explain.

"Cotton warps were used widely in the worsted branches from the 1830s, and the typical product of the Bradford area became a cotton warp-worsted weft cloth. In addition, the woollen branch used recovered wool and silk, the latter for use especially in the manufacture of waistcoats and striped materials.

"The worsted industry also used a limited amount of silk in combination with alpaca. Alpaca and mohair increased the range of 19th Century 'lustre cloths', combining alpaca or mohair with cotton warps brought huge success to firms like Salts of Saltaire...

"As well as producing finished cloth, the Yorkshire industry sold large quantities of yarn. Worsted cloths were produced in mills for local consumption in the early 19th Century and were increasingly sold abroad as Europe and the USA developed their own manufacturing sectors, often behind a tariff shield."

Before the adoption of steam power, mills were comparatively simple and relatively small. The introduction of steam engines to power machinery in textile factories had the effect of increasing both the number and the size of Yorkshire Mills, as well as the number of people operating the machines. Giles and Goodall again:-

"Even in 1834 the average workforce in a wool textile mill was less than 50. It would be wrong, therefore, to imagine that the Yorkshire industry was characterised by a thorough-going 'factory system' in this early period...

"The picture altered radically after 1825. The most important development was the achievement of fully mechanised production in virtually all aspects of the industry. The principal innovation was the power-loom, largely unsuccessful before 1825, but applied to all branches, albeit at different rates, thereafter.

"The other major developments were the introduction of powered mule spinning in the woollen branch in the 1820s and of machine combing in the worsted industry in the mid-19th Century.

"In all branches, less far-reaching but still significant advances were made. Technical innovations allowed a wider range of products to be made by machines which became larger, worked more quickly and were increasingly automatic and therefore labour saving.

"A large increase in factory employment is clearly marked in this period. In the woollen branch the number of mills increased from 406 in 1835 to 998 in 1874. In the worsted branch there were 204 mills in 1835 but 570 in 1874." Worsted mills were much larger than woollen mills.

This then is the industrial background of mid-Victorian England when Titus Salt, after much trial and error, came up with a new idea.

"From what was a useless material he has built up a great industry which has for many years in his own model town supported several thousand people whose life has been happier by comforts and institutions which many a larger community would gladly boast of..."

This breathless eulogy in the Engineer magazine on January 5th 1877 correctly underlined the importance of that unidentified "useless material" in the fortunes of Titus Salt. The material in question, of course, was alpaca; considered superior to English wool in length, softness and pliability. Salt was the first manufacturer to spin it into an even thread, combine it with cotton and silk warps, and create a new staple industry.

Alpaca belonged to the Llama tribe of sheep and lived in the mountains of Peru. Its hair of various shades, including black, brown, grey and white, was remarkable for its lustre and softness.

Salt had already successfully spun Russian wool into yarn and woven the yarn into cloth at Thompson's Mill in Bradford's Silsbridge Lane (now Grattan Road) when, in 1836, during a business trip to Liverpool, he chanced to enter the quayside warehouse of Hagan and Co., and saw more than 300 bales of Peruvian wool gathering dust. Salt, ever on the lookout for something new, was curious about the unrefined hair which nobody else wanted.

According to Salt's 19th Century biographer Robert Balgarnie, he returned to the warehouse at a later date and this time took a sample of the "useless material" back to Bradford. His instinct had been right. But Salt, ever prudent, wanted to be sure of the fibre's commercial potential.

The story goes that the 33-year-old shut himself up in one of his Bradford mills, washed and dried the sample hair himself, combed it out, then measured its length, strength and quality. Jack Reynolds takes up the story:-

"Along with a small team of trusted assistants, Salt had been working in great secrecy for about 18 months on the problems which alpaca presented. By adapting the machinery available, they had between them overcome the difficulties of spinning the material into a true and even thread...

"Salt and his team had the idea of binding alpaca weft with cotton or silk warps; and this gave the characteristic lustre which made it an attractive cloth, and produced at the same time a durable, relatively light and reasonably priced cloth which could be easily adapted to the fashions of the day."   In 1834, when Salt set up in business, alpaca imports amounted to a mere 5,700 lbs. Six years later that had grown to an avalanche: 1,325,000 lbs, most of it arriving in the West Riding by canal barge and cart. For about a quarter of a century from 1840, bright alpaca mixed-fabrics took the world by storm.

For more than 25 years Salt had worked in the dirty heart of bursting-at-the-seams Bradford. As the American Harpers New Monthly magazine was to observe: "By his 45th year he was a very rich man, and might have retired with a lordly income, establishing himself in some fertile and umbrageous domain, deserted by a spendthrift noble, among the merchant princes of Yorkshire..." But Salt had other ideas.

He was proposing to abandon Bradford for a green field site more than three miles to the north. Everything was based in town. Yet Salt proposed removing to the country, putting himself to the astronomical expense of building a vast new works, fire-proof and with all modern conveniences.

Expansion and prosperity had at last in 1846 brought Bradford its railway link with London, via Leeds. The route lay through Shipley, at one point converging on the Leeds-Liverpool canal and the River Aire. Passenger-carrying trains could also transport merchandise, Salt reasoned. Manufacturing in overcrowded, unhealthy and dangerous surroundings was no longer necessary; all the separate processes of worsted-making could be gathered together in one place, out in the country.

Although Salt could have packed his money bags and retired to a green spa or blue

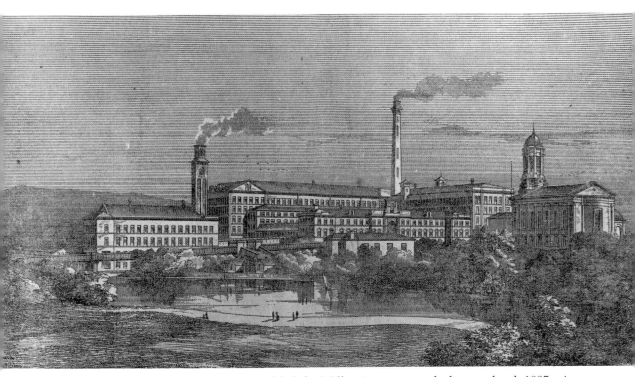

One of the wonders of the industrial world: Salts Mill in its green and pleasant land, 1885, nine years after Salt's death. *Courtesy: Bradford Libraries*

coast, merely to die a millionaire was not an end in itself in his scale of values. A down-to-earth realist in business, Salt had a dream which he believed was his God-given duty to turn into reality. And so on a chilly November evening in 1849 Salt, the Mayor of Bradford, walked into the comfortable fire-lit chambers of architects Lockwood and Mawson.

Henry Francis Lockwood, born in Doncaster in 1811, had gained his credentials in London and then in 1834 (the year that Salt started his own business and the year of William Morris's birth), opened his first office in Hull - later the birthplace of Jonathan Silver's father Sydney.

Lockwood's decision to move to Bradford was not fortuitous. In the words of the Athenaeum magazine, Bradford was "the youngest and rawest child of the industrial revolution". There was any amount of new building to be done. What was fortunate, however, was Lockwood's decision to team up with William Mawson, a 21-year-old bachelor from Leeds, and his brother Richard. The firm of Lockwood and Mawson was to design Bradford's most memorable buildings - the ones that survived Stanley Wardley's bulldozers in the late 1950s and early 1960s.

Salt had sounded out another architect, George Knowles, but changed his mind. He was impressed by Lockwood and Mawson's success in winning the contract to design St George's Hall.

Salt consulted his banker, Henry Harris, chairman of the Bradford Old Bank, the most respected banking company in the town (later to become part of Barclays - Jonathan Silver's bankers). He then went to Lockwood and Mawson's new chambers with the sketch of an idea for a gigantic worsted mill on the banks of the canal.

Their preliminary drawing did not please Salt, it was too small; he wanted something larger with a facade like Osborne House, Queen Victoria's favourite residence on the Isle of Wight. Lockwood told him such a building would cost at least £100,000. Salt did not demur. His reply, typically laconic, was in effect 'do it'. The firm proceeded to design the most advanced, fully integrated mill in Yorkshire if not Europe.

It was not the most unusual, however. That title surely belongs to the flax mill built in 1838-40 in Holbeck in Leeds, a two-acre factory with an ancient Egyptian facade modelled on the temple of Horus at Edfu. Nevertheless, the grandeur of Salts, set between tree-covered hills and water, was fulsomely acknowledged by The Practical Magazine in 1874, whose anonymous correspondent said the building rivalled if not exceeded every other industrial establishment of the same description in the UK.

A traveller on the Midland Railway, passing the new palace of industry, would have been struck first of all by the 250-ft chimney with its decorated cornice. His eye would have been dazzled by the four decks of windows reflecting sunlight along the 230-yard length of its south-facing facade. He would have wondered at the two Italianate bell towers. As the train slowed as it approached the small station our imaginary traveller might have glimpsed Titus Salt's carriage turning left off Victoria Road into the stables, or even seen his tall, bearded-figure going up the small flight of stone steps to his own private door in the office block. He would not have seen the vast subterranean reservoir, partly fed by rainwater which passed through the mill by a system of pipes. He may have read about the ten huge boilers and the two pairs of beam engines powering this mighty edifice. With the help of William Fairburn, the leading civil engineer of the day, Salt ensured that his "works" was not only beautiful to look at but was as safe as money and ingenuity could make it. Brick and cast iron reduced the risk of fire internally - the commonest hazard of mills - and drive shafts of some of the machinery were placed under the floor to reduce the risk of mutilating accidents.

But what was going on inside? The American magazine Harpers New Monthly gave its 19th Century readers the following detailed description.

"Twelve hundred looms are contained in the factory, which are capable of producing 30,000 yards of alpaca cloth daily, or some 5,688 miles of it a year, which, as the crow flies, would reach from Saltaire over the land and the sea to Peru, the native mountains of the alpaca sheep.

"The alpaca wool reaches the manufacturer in what are called ballots or small bales each weighing 125 lbs (Donskoi wool arrived in 300 lb. bags, and mohair in 180 lb. bags). The bale consists of fleeces which are sorted into from six to ten different qualities, adapted for the various grades of manufacture.

"The primary processes are sorting, washing, drying, plucking, combing, drawing, roving, spinning, weaving, dyeing, pressing, finishing, and folding (13 processes in

The palace of industry about to become a palace of culture and commerce. The Saltaire Ltd part of the sign has been removed.
Photo: Salts Estates

all), exclusive of reeling, sizing and warping - common to all worsted manufacture.

"After the sorting, washing and drying, the various qualities go into the hands of the comber, the washing having been done by the rollers especially adapted for the purpose, and operated by steam-power.

"The beautiful variety of shades is obtained by an admixture of the 'sliverings' which shows a thorough union of the inherent colours of the raw material, and so combines them to give the finished stuffs a delicacy and gentle blending of shade and tints unequalled by any other worsted fabric.

"Each weaver passes over about three pieces of the better qualities, of forty yards each, weekly, and more of the inferior qualities. After leaving the weaver, the stuffs are examined by the 'taker-in', who looks for defects in the weaving. Then it is folded up into what are called 'pieces' to be sent to the dyer, although usually the goods are sold to the merchants who themselves employ the dyer.

"The white cloths are sent to the dyer to receive the various colours, while the 'self' colours pass immediately into the finisher's hands, who puts them through the processes of steaming, singeing, crabbing, dyeing, and pressing - these imparting to the cloth its glossy quality, and preventing it from shrinking.

"When the manufacturer or merchant receives the goods duly dyed and finished, they are measured, made up and folded in paper, ready for export or delivery to the draper."

The mill was formally opened on Tuesday, September 20th, 1853 - Titus Salt's 50th birthday. Salt laid on a gargantuan feast for 3,500 workers in the combing shed. They consumed two tons of meat, half-a-ton of potatoes, 420 plum puddings and jellies, as well as mountains of grapes, melons, peaches, pineapples, nectarines and apricots - food which most factory workers never saw in a lifetime.

Commenting on the inaugural blow-out, the Illustrated London News said it was "probably the largest dinner party ever set down under one roof at one time." More food was served at that feast than on the first evening of the Titanic's fatal maiden voyage.

One September Sunday 140 years later this same combing shed was the setting for Poetry or Bust, a witty morality play in verse by poet and dramatist Tony Harrison. It was the story of the notorious drunk, poet, and sometime employee of Titus Salt - John Nicholson. On August 24th 1995, almost 142 years after Titus Salt's inaugural banquet, Pace Micro Technology invited nearly 700 people to a celebratory buffet lunch in this same shed. Past and present had come full circle.

Titus Salt's 18-month tussle with that "useless material" alpaca, his decision to leave dirty industrial Bradford behind, had paid off. He had come up with a new idea for manufacturing at a time of change and innovation. His greatest achievements, however, were still to come.

5. DARK SATANIC MILLTOWN

Thirty-two years after the first factory act for workhouse children the Poor Law was amended. The year, 1834, also saw the death of the Rev. Robert Malthus whose book, Principle of Population (the sixth edition had been published in 1826), helped create the climate of opinion which made the Poor Law so harsh.

Malthus, a precursor of the doomsday ecologists of our own time, alarmed the well-to-do by painting a picture of a rapidly multiplying lower class devouring the country's available food stocks like a plague of locusts. Measures had to be taken to ensure that they did not flourish. The unemployed, the unwanted, the un-self-sufficient were driven by need into crime (for which they could be hung, jailed or transported) or the parish workhouses. Workhouses were deliberately "uninviting places of wholesome restraint".

Thirty-two Guardians were appointed in Bradford to administer this system of harsh charity. Joseph Fieldhouse gives a vivid account of the unpopularity of the Poor Law regime in his history of Bradford.

"The general policy was to give relief only to those who entered workhouses, which were so like prisons they were known as 'Bastilles'. Here the object was to make life so unpleasant that men would gladly accept the lowest wages to get out, and a man separated from wife and family was under intolerable pressure to do so." Such was the swell of hatred for Bradford's Guardians that in November 1837 the courthouse where they were holding forth was besieged by 6,000 angry poor. The Riot Act was read and 40 Hussars sent to restore order with the flats of their sabre blades.

Oliver Twist, published in Bentley's Miscellany between February 1837 and April 1839, is tellingly subtitled the Parish Boy's Progress. Some people now regard Dickens as a bit quaint; but which novelist in our own age has written with such restrained and literate gusto about a social evil?

"They established the rule, that all poor people should have the alternative (for they would compel nobody, not they) of being starved by a gradual process in the house or by a quick one out of it. With this view they contracted with the water-works to lay on an unlimited supply of water; and with a corn factor to supply periodically small quantities of oatmeal; and issued three meals of this gruel a day, with an onion twice a week, and half a roll on Sundays. They made a great many other wise and humane regulations, having reference to the ladies, which it is not necessary to repeat; kindly

A place of dirt and squalor. No wonder Salt built his new mill on a green-field site out of town.

Courtesy: Bradford Libraries

undertook to divorce poor married people, in consequence of the great expense of a suit in Doctors' Commons; and, instead of compelling a man to support his family, as they had heretofore done, took his family away from him, and made him a bachelor!"

For many life was indeed nasty, brutish and short. Bradford's infant mortality was the fifth highest in the country. Disease was rife. In 1849, the very year Salt made up his mind to transfer his business to the green pastures of the River Aire, a cholera epidemic killed 426 people in Bradford.

Anti-slavery reformers such as Richard Oastler campaigned long and hard for a shorter working week for children.

They had a measure of success in 1833 when children aged nine to 12 in textile factories were limited to nine hours a day (no more than 48 in a working week). Another nine years passed before legislation prohibited women, girls and boys under ten from working underground in collieries. Thomas Mackley gave evidence to the Children's Employment Commission in 1842 about conditions for nine girls in mines in Wilsden "They have a chain or belt about the waist, which passes between the legs of the female, and is hooked to the wagon of coals (the corves), which they pull from the place where the men work... all the men in the pit were perfectly naked." Joseph Fieldhouse says children went down into dangerous shafts regularly at the age of five; many at seven, but most at eight. "One collier at Birkenshaw was known to have his own child to 'hurry' at three..."

Sceptics say Titus Salt left Bradford to avoid paying local taxes. Even supposing the accusation to be true, Salt had lived and worked in the heart of the town long enough to be familiar with the multiple side-effects of unregulated industrialisation.

In 1845, James Smith reported on the sanitary conditions of booming Bradford.

"The water of this basin is so often charged with decaying matter, that in hot weather bubbles of sulphated hydrogen are continually rising to the surface, and so much is the atmosphere loaded with gas, that watch-cases and other materials of silver become black in the pockets of the workmen employed near the canal. The stench is sometimes very strong and fevers prevail all around. Taking the general condition of Bradford, I am obliged to pronounce it to be the filthiest town I have ever visited." The canal, known as River Stink, resembled that seething dye-discoloured nightmare polluting Coketown in Dickens' Hard Times. Fifteen years after Smith's much quoted pronouncement, the canal basin had become so stagnant and offensive with industrial effluent that boys were said to ignite the toxic vapour it gave off at night, using lighted tapers fastened to poles. Belatedly, an order was made forbidding the Bradford Canal Company from using the polluted waters of the Beck.

We have a first-hand account of dirty Bradford and working conditions for the majority of the population.

On December 13th, 1849, The Bradford Observer published 'Impressions of Bradford' by a special correspondent of the Morning Chronicle. "Bradford is essentially a new town," it began. The population was estimated to be 132,000 much greater than the usual figure quoted for 1851 of 107,000.

"Trade is at present exceedingly brisk in Bradford - so brisk that even stables are put into requisition to contain the wool, for lack of ware-house room. The number of persons, therefore, receiving parish relief is comparatively small, and, excepting an isolated case or two, I am told that not one single native of this town is upon the books. The paupers are mainly Irish and English agricultural labourers who have not as yet learned to be useful in their new sphere." Edwin Chadwick's Poor Law amendment was evidently having the desired effect.

The Morning Chronicle goes on: "Bradford may be described as an accumulation of main streets, steep lanes and huge mills - intersected here and there by those odious patches of black, muddy waste ground, rooted up by pigs, and strewed with oyster shells, cabbage stalks, and such garbage, which I have so often noticed as commonly existing in manufacturing towns.

"Since Mr Smith of Deanston passed sentence upon Bradford the Corporation, although they might have done more, have not been idle. Upwards of 30 streets and lanes have been paved and drained, and some of the worst Irish Colonies have been materially improved...

"Cellars are very numerous in Bradford, and not one operative family in a hundred possesses more than two rooms - 'a house and a chamber'. In respect of dwelling accommodation the worst feature of the stuff and woollen towns is, that they seem to be making little or no progress. In the case of ranges of houses, even of a comparatively superior class, the privies are built in clusters, in a small space, left open behind, instead of each being placed in a quiet, decent situation, close to the house to which it belongs." The correspondent inspected some 'low Irish haunts'; a few of the inhabitants were woolcombers, but mostly they were hawkers.

"The average earnings of the hawkers they started as from 1s to 1/6d a day (5p to 7.5p). Their houses almost always consisted of a single room - generally a cellar - a low, dark, foul smelling place, with rough stools and a broken table or so lying about; coarse crockery, either unwashed or full of dirty water; knives without handles, and forks with broken prongs; bits of loaves smeared over by dirty hands; bundles of rags, buckets of slops, and unmade beds huddled on the stone or earthen floor in corners. There always seems to exist a sort of community of dwellings among these people which I never find amongst their English neighbours." In Silsbridge Lane a family of nine in one room had only one bed between them. In Westgate 13 people, including four women, shared two bundles of straw.

"In a lodging-house which I saw, there was bed room for 16 at 3d each; that is to say there were four frames covered with rags in the lower room, and the same accommodation in the higher. The single men slept by themselves. Married couples and single women occupied the other apartment jointly. There could not, when I called, have been less than a dozen men and women smoking round the fire."

"I think we deserve to be beaten out of our beautiful houses with a scourge of small cords - all of us who let tenants live in such sties as we see around us," says Dorothea

Brooke in George Eliot's novel Middlemarch. "Life in cottages might be happier than ours, if they were real houses fit for human beings from whom we expect duties and affections".

Bradford's first main drain was not begun until 1863. Three years later the Corporation was still trying to raise £120,000 to construct main sewers.

Friedrich Engels, who had written about the conditions of Manchester's working class in the 1840s, called Bradford a "stinking hole", which it was, crammed with coal-fired mills, dye works, iron foundries, chemical and grease works, vitriol, soap and gas works. Frequently cloud-covered and smog-filled. On rainy days Bradford was also enveloped in the rancid odour of wet fleeces.

The cheapest route out of Bradford was via a tankard, jug or bottle. By 1868 no fewer than 750 beer houses and inns were supplying the town. The quality of the water supply was made dangerous to health by the chemical compounds pouring into the air from factories and the toxic mixtures seeping into the water table. In the throat-burning atmosphere of industrial Bradford beer and gin were probably safer to drink.

Howard Spring's novel Fame is the Spur, the story of the rise of the Labour Party (founded in Bradford), describes the city in the latter years of the century. No fictional, thinly disguised Bruddersford of J.B. Priestley's Bright Day: Spring describes real places.

"The needs of the people were bare before their eyes in that town compacted of mills and factories, warehouses, back-to-back dwellings climbing the steep streets, built in the riotous hey-day of the industrial revolution when the housing of the 'hands' was a matter of less thought than the kennelling of dogs. Nothing had ever been done about it. The impetus of the great industrial change-over from hand loom weaving in the homes, with pure streams flowing by the doorstep, to factory production, and polluted rivers, and congregated thousands in dwellings that were ugly to begin with and now were squalid, and filthily insanitary: that impetus still rolled wool-making Bradford along - the town of the golden fleece - pleasant to live in, as Lizzie said at breakfast that day, if you were fleecing and not being fleeced."

The life of home-based hand loom weavers living on the hills around Bradford may have been idyllic as Spring describes; but for many of the 15,000 woolcombers in 1849, those working outside the factory system, life was hell on earth judging by the Morning Chronicle's correspondent.

"These men sometimes work singly, but more often three or four or five club together and labour in what is called a shop, generally consisting of an upper room or 'chamber' over the lower room or 'house'. Their wives and children assist them to a certain extent in the first and almost unskilled portions of the operation, but the whole process is crude and easily acquired.

"It consists of forcibly pulling the wool through metal combs or spikes of different lengths, and set five or six deep. These combs must be kept at a high temperature, and consequently the central apparatus in a combing room is always a 'fire pot' burning either coke, coals, or charcoal, and constructed so as to allow three, four or five combs to be heated at it - the vessel being in these cases respectively called a 'pot o' three', 'pot o' four', or 'pot o' five'...

"The general aspect of the combing room may therefore be described as that of a bare chamber, heated to nearly 85 degrees. A round fire pot stands in the centre; the masses of wool are heaped about; and four or five men in their shirt sleeves, are working busily." He goes on to describe the atmosphere of one of these musty chambers filled with burning charcoal fumes.

Charcoal was often used, usually at the insistence of the 'master'. The journalist met a sick man combing mohair by means of charcoal-heated combs. He worked from 6am until 10pm. He and his wife had seven children, five of whom slept in a single bed. Three of them worked in a mill, earning a total of 12 shillings (60p) a week.

Irish immigrants were regarded with suspicion by the indigenous working population. The Morning Chronicle's man was told they were willing to work for less than the going rate, thus undercutting everyone else. He then recounts at length the story of an Irish woman whose home for herself and her four children was poor but immaculately kept.

Her husband had been a hand loom weaver. He had died of consumption and his widow was given 29 shillings (£1.45p) by the parish of Menston and told to seek work and shelter in Bradford.

"The people at the mill were very kind, much kinder than the farmers. They took the little boy and set him to easy work, and gave him 2 shillings (10p) a week. Then the manager said I might come into the mill and see him, and try if I couldn't learn to do something myself. So I got to know how to pick lumps out of the slubbings, and first I got 5/6d, and last week I was raised to 6 shillings so we now have 9 shillings a week.

"Well, first I lived in a room belonging to the mill, with an outside stair, and I paid ls rent. But I was afraid of the children breaking their necks there. The only other place I could get near the mill was this. There are two rooms here and the rent is 2 shillings. I know it's too much for the likes of me to pay; but I think of the children. Well, sir, the parish are very good to me, and give me 3 shillings a week - 2 shillings for the rent and l shilling for coals - and we live and clothe ourselves on the other eight shillings.

"We live chiefly on bread. I get a stone-and-a-half of flour every week, and I bake it on Sundays. Then we have a little tea or coffee and sometimes we have a little offal meat, because it's cheap.

"A good gentleman gave me the furniture I have and the bed in the other room. It cost altogether 15 shillings. Every body has been very kind to me, and the neighbours come in often to look after the children when I'm at work. I was born in Shandon Parish, in Cork; and oh! I wish there were mills there for the poor people to work in. It would be a blessing to them indeed!"

A prolonged and bitter strike at Lister's Mill in 1891, in which thousands were locked out for protesting against a cut in wages, gave rise to the founding of the Independent Labour Party two years later. George Bernard Shaw was among those who journeyed to Bradford in January 1893 to launch the precursor of the modern Labour Party.

6. A SOCIAL FABRIC

"It is physically impossible for a well-educated, intellectual, or brave man to make money the chief object of his thoughts."

John Ruskin, the author of that quote, might have been talking about the working class; more probably, he had in mind those uncouth captains of industry for whom money was less a means to an end than an end in itself. If by well-educated Ruskin meant a classical education at university, Titus Salt was not well-educated. Nor was Salt an intellectual: he tried to solve problems rather than talk or write about them. As for bravery, his willingness to intervene during one of the Bradford riots is testimony to that. Salt also had the courage of his convictions, moral bravery. But what do we know of his attitude to money?

Victorians who rose from a humble background to great wealth, acclaim and social status knew the value of money: it was a good servant but a bad master. Salt believed money was a tool to be put to work for the general good. At a time when it was usual for very rich men to show off their wealth by purchasing large estates or building mansions, Salt was an exception to the rule. The only mansion he ever built was Salts Mill, his "works". He did not even buy his own home until he was 63. However, he encouraged others to build homes for themselves.

"Like his Halifax friends, Edward Akroyd and John Crossley, Salt showed considerable interest in improved workers' housing," states the 1987 Bradford Antiquary. "In 1849 he was the first President of the Bradford Freehold Land Society which enabled 'a man in humble circumstances to acquire a piece of land, paying for it by monthly instalments, with a view to the ultimate erection of a dwelling in which to live'. Several streets of back-to-back housing in Bradford resulted from this activity." Salt and his friends had organised a building society.

Between 1851 and 1871 Salt spent £170,000 building homes for his workers, and sundry amenities which he considered essential for a healthy and civilised life. These included a row of 14 shops on Victoria Road (the village had 40 by 1871), a public baths and wash house on Caroline Street (the former had 24 baths for men and women, the latter contained six washing machines, wringers, and a heated drying closet). Salts spent nearly as much again building 45 almshouses, a three-ward hospital, a high school for girls and boys, and a multi-purpose club and institute. After 1870 he added 11 acres of landscaped park on the other side of the River Aire, where

Salt had a cranky dislike of lines of washing in his model village, as this watercolour by Simon Palmer shows.

Courtesy: Simon Palmer & Jonathan Silver

his workers might stroll, play cricket, tennis, bowls, or even practise archery.

He gave away many thousands of pounds to charities and worthy causes he considered deserving during his lifetime, and in his will left an endowment of £30,000 for the sick and aged poor of Saltaire.

The following story by Robert Balgarnie, Salt's biographer, throws the sharpest light on the industrialist's attitude to surplus wealth.

One day Salt and Henry Lockwood visited Lord Harewood, Lord Lieutenant of the County, to invite him to attend the grand opening of Salts Mill. Over lunch, Lord Harewood said: "How is it Mr Salt that you do not invest your capital in landed property and enjoy the remainder of your life free from the strain of business?"

Salt's reported reply (alas there are too few of them) epitomises the difference between the class which thought itself born to rule, and God-fearing capitalist dissenters - chapel radicals, like himself. "In the first place, I thought that by the concentration of my works in one locality I might provide occupation for my sons. Moreover, as a landed proprietor I felt I should be out of my element ... outside of my business I am nothing, in it I have considerable influence. By the opening of Saltaire I also hope to do good to my fellow man."

Benjamin Disraeli's novel Coningsby, published in 1844, contains an uncanny description of a model village, uncanny because it seems to presage what was to appear at Saltaire in the 20 years from 1851.

"A village of not inconsiderable size, and remarkable from the neatness and even picturesque character of the architecture and the gay gardens that surround it. This village had a church, a parsonage, a school house, and an institute containing a library, lecture room and reading room." Salt may have drawn his inspiration from Disraeli. However, the idea for Salt's model industrial community was more than likely conceived over a period longer than that which is required to read a novel. Besides, Salt wasn't given to novel-reading.

The cholera epidemic in 1849 may have spurred Salt on to remove his works to a healthier location. An example of what could be done was to be found in neighbouring Halifax. Copley Mill in the Calder Valley, had its own model village which doubtless inspired Edward Akroyd in 1847 to commission his own. Akroydan was finished in about 1856.

Titus Salt did not originate the concept of the model village, as some people think; he was following a trail blazed by others, his friend Akroyd for instance, David Dale, founder of New Lanark in Scotland, and Robert Owen.

Dale, born on January 6th, 1739, was apprenticed as a hand loom weaver in Paisley, the centre of West Scotland's textile and fashion industry. He started cotton spinning in four mills at New Lanark in 1786, providing day and evening schooling for the children.

By the 1790s Dale employed more than 1,100 people of whom nearly 800 were children. There were 275 pauper apprentices from Glasgow and Edinburgh whose home was Number 4 mill. Writing, figuring, sewing and church music were taught by 16 teachers. Dale died in 1806.

Robert Owen, the Welsh saddler's son usually credited with creating New Lanark, did not go there until 1811 or so when he was in his early thirties. Owen, who had borrowed £100 to go into business on his own account in Manchester, was an experienced industrial manager.

At the age of 21 he was in charge of a factory employing 500 people, spinning Sea Island cotton imported from the southern states of America. Immorality, vice and crime prevailed in mills in those early, unregulated years of industrialisation, according to Jacob Bronowski and Bruce Mazlish.

"Drunkenness and laziness cut down productivity. Thievery was widespread, and turbulent and degenerate conditions of life were rife. Adults and children alike existed in misery, working long hours for little money, constantly living in squalid surroundings. Uneducated, uncared for, they were given less consideration than the

Almshouses for Salt's retired workers. His social fabric preceded the Welfare State and demonstrated real care in the community.   *Photo: Salts Estates*

machines they tended...

"He (Owen) started a school for children under five. Further, he provided all his workers with better housing, clothing and food, instituted a health fund and, skilfully, through his ability to handle workmen, eliminated the causes of drunkenness, theft and fornication. After 16 years of persevering in these measures, Owen had, as he himself claimed, "effected a complete change in the general character of the village".

Owen sailed to America to spread the gospel in 1825, founding New Harmony in Indiana. He passionately believed that character was formed by social conditions.

"Man is born with a desire to obtain happiness, which desire is the primary cause of all his actions," he said. He had set out his social philosophy in 1813 in A New View of Society: or Essays on the Principles of the Formation of the Human Character and the Application of the Principle to the Practice.

"Any general character, from the best to the worst, from the most ignorant to the most enlightened, may be given to any community, even to the world at large, by the application of proper means, which means are to a great extent at the command and under the control of those who have influence in the affairs of men."

The idea that character was formed by environment irrespective of free will could not explain, however, the rise of a man like Titus Salt. Although he did not go as far as Owen in creating a commune, in effect a kibbutz, Salt accepted the Welshman's fundamental principle that a bad environment may thwart and perhaps pervert the pursuit of happiness.

The difference between Salt and Owen was that the Yorkshireman wanted to create a beautiful industrial community rather than a Utopian settlement where the collective took priority over the individual. Salt believed in free will, and was a practical man of business before he was an idealist. He was a practical Utopian.

Nowadays Saltaire is commuter-belt territory. The snug houses are increasingly sought after by young professional couples working in the media or local government. A record of tenants in 1871 shows that during Salt's lifetime Saltaire was occupied largely by industrial workers.

At 36 Ada Street lived Benjamin and Ruth Smithson, both 40. He was a delver, she was a weaver. Their 15-year-old son Thomas was a spinner. The couple also had a baby daughter, Ellen, and a daughter-in-law of 15 as well as a step-daughter of 14. The former was a weaver, the latter a spinner.

Of the eight occupants of 44 Ada Street, the home of Jeremiah Whiteoak and his wife Margaret, three worked as weavers and one as a spinner. The master of the house was a tailor.

At 23 Whitlam Street, John Smith, a warehouseman, and his wife Mary, lived with their four children. The eldest two, Harriet, 15, and Martha, 13, were both worsted spinners.

A family of ten shared 5 Helen Street, home of Joshua and Sarah Laycock, both 53. He was unemployed, but five other members of the household (which included two nephews, one niece and two sons-in-law) brought home a weekly wage.

Rents ranged from two shillings and fourpence (15p) to seven and six (37.5p).

Saltaire, says Jack Reynolds, was "Salt's personal response to the pressures urging peace and stability between Capital and Labour which emerged in the aftermath of Chartism." The 1830s and 1840s were volatile and hazardous. "The political dangers of the period sharpened the point of view, for everywhere the working classes in the process of dissolution and reformation threatened widespread political instability. The town was the principal arena for their struggles."

What Reynolds calls "the physical and moral anarchy of the industrial town" was aided and abetted by the proliferation of taverns and pubs as well as environmental squalor. Salt had served as a magistrate and was well aware of the effect of drink on lives that were irredeemably hard.

Owen had his followers, however. John Minter Morgan and James S. Buckingham both lectured in Bradford, Morgan in 1850 and Buckingham in 1846.

Buckingham and Morgan both proposed the creation of model settlements. In 1844 the Society for Improving the Condition of the Labouring Classes was formed, and in the following year the Metropolitan Society for Improving the Dwellings of the Industrial Classes. Within ten years there were 20 such associations in different parts of the country.

Attribute whatever motive you like to Salt for building Saltaire, the fact remains that he did not have to do it. As Lord Harewood remarked he was rich enough to live a life of leisure and luxury. Salt however, had no use for leisure and luxury. He enjoyed the comforts which affluence brought, but believed that his duty was to enhance the spiritual well-being of working people by improving their material lot.

"Salt's new mill and village were to be everything Bradford was not. They were designed to nurture self-improvement, politeness, orderly behaviour, and good health among his workers. Salt's aim was to construct a successful company village, separate from the town, organised and ordered according to these objectives. In so doing he intended to demonstrate that factories, the Capitalist free market, and the amassing of great industrial fortunes like his own were compatible with material comfort and moral virtue among the working classes.

"They were to be shown that great wealth carried great responsibilities; that it was the Christian duty of the virtuous employer to promote the material and moral well being of his work people and his town," says John Styles in his booklet Titus Salt & Saltaire: Industry and Virtue.

In 1856, three years after the opening of Salts Mill, Salt's workers presented their employer with a marble bust of himself, "as a tribute of our love". Love, mark you. How many bosses in today's dog-eat-dog world could claim the love of their workers? Salt declared a holiday and transported by train more than 2,000 of them to his home at Lightcliffe where, under large marquees, they sat down to another enormous feast.

On receipt of the bust at St George's Hall that evening, Salt gave a short speech in which he twice referred to his self-appointed task of improving the condition of the working classes - unconsciously paraphrasing the title of Engels' book of 1845: the Condition of the English Working Classes.

Some of the 29 streets of Salt's model village with its 850 stone-built homes.   *Photo: Salts Estates*

"I advocated the Reform Bill of 1832 ... I supported the successful effort to repeal the Corn Laws and for the extension of education among the working classes ... I shall support the vote by ballot," he added. Private wealth and public action: that was the heart of Salt's vision, the flame that burned.

Architecture, said art historian Kenneth Clark, reveals more about civilisation than either painting or literature; it is a more "communal art" involving a relationship between the user and the maker.

We tend to forget that building beautifully and building functionally were not always thought of as incompatible. Nowadays buildings are like sculptures, regarded as artistic artefacts irrespective of whether they actually work as buildings.

John Ruskin, son of a prosperous wine merchant, a man of private means, inspired the poet and artist William Morris to found the Society for the Preservation of Ancient Buildings. "When we build, let us think that we build for ever," Ruskin had proclaimed.

The quality of public buildings, especially housing, concerned him deeply. Politically inclined towards Socialism, he was mistrustful of laissez-faire Liberals like Titus Salt. He regarded the great enterprise at Saltaire with scepticism; paternalistic philanthropy was no substitute for properly co-ordinated state action to provide suitable homes throughout the country. Housing was too important to be left to the whim of millionaire businessmen like Salt, Edward Akroyd, or any other do-gooder.

The industrial landscapes of Northern England were grim and dirty; but the closeness of the houses to each other and to the place of work at least preserved a human dimension. The painter L.S. Lowry captured this in what he called his "dream-scapes" of the streets of Oldham, Salford and Manchester.

Ruskin lectured twice in Bradford. The first occasion was in 1859 when he spoke on manufacture and design. I shall return to that later in this chapter. Ruskin's second visit in April 1864, the year his father died and left him £120,000, had to do with buildings. He was invited to talk on the subject of the art of designing and constructing noble buildings.

Like Prince Charles today, Ruskin passionately believed that the shape and appearance of a building, any building, profoundly affected the social fabric. He added his weight to the public controversy over Lockwood and Mawson's Italianate design for Bradford's proposed Wool Exchange. He thought it was too elaborate.

The proposed Wool Exchange was to be the town's first public edifice made out of locally quarried sandstone. It was a sign of the times, as Malcolm Hardman says: "Bradford had blossomed more suddenly than most towns, and from more sternly Puritanical roots ... In the respectable streets of the Bradford Ruskin visited, buildings of stern and squat vernacular style were being shouldered aside by raw edifices in the grand Italian manner."   Ruskin's preference was for the Gothic, which shows the difference in outlook between a man of inherited means like himself and the self-made manufacturers of Bradford. To the latter, or at least to the architects who designed their buildings, the Renaissance style symbolised the triumph of man. To Ruskin, however, it represented vanity; self-glorification. Ruskin believed that man should glory in God and His Creation, not in himself.

Lockwood and Mawson's design won the day, however. J.B. Priestley's favourite building in Market Street (his favourite thoroughfare) joined other "raw edifices" like St. George's Hall, which was completed in 1853 - the same year as Salts Mill. But the concert hall was made from fine grey sandstone from the Park Spring Quarry near Leeds, a duller substance than Yorkshire Stone.

The windows of the room where I am writing this look out across the valley to the Spion Kop of earth excavated from the quarry where the stone for Salts Mill was cut.

"The sight of fresh-cut Bradford sandstone, of an indefinable pale, strong gold against the kind of blue West Riding sky - such would be Ruskin's view of Bradfordian possibilities as he first passed Saltaire on his way into Bradford from Bolton Abbey," writes Malcolm Hardman.

"Here were materials fit for a New Jerusalem: a sharp contrast to the millstone grit of Halifax to the West, which rapidly turns black on exposure to air; a contrast to the sooty brick of Leeds immediately to the East."   A contrast too, he could have added, to the grey granite canyons of Edinburgh and the red brick of municipal Manchester. The pale gold of Yorkshire Stone complementing the Matisse blueness of the sky (on bright days), is an integral part of Bradford's industrial heritage.

Sadly, many of the city's grand 19th Century buildings were bulldozed during that brash epoch of Room at the Top and Billy Liar in the late 1950s and early 1960s. David Hockney sketched some of pre-1960s Bradford, perhaps sensing that he was recording part of Bradford which in a few short years would be 'improved' out of existence by misguided council officials and corrupt architects like the late John Poulson.

Fittingly, Hockney's city-scapes are now hanging from the steam pipes which used to heat Titus Salt's spinning mill - now Jonathan Silver's 1853 Gallery.

In March 1859, Ruskin was invited to Bradford by the newly-opened Bradford School of Design, set up to further the cause of art for its own sake and the technical benefits it could bestow. The topic under discussion was manufacture and design.

"He was not preaching to an audience of ignorant philistines," says Malcolm Hardman, "but to one of the liveliest and most intelligent communities of the 19th Century."

If measured from the start of railways in 1825, industrialisation on a significant scale was less than 40 years old. Technological advance had been rapid, creating a material need and then supplying it in abundance. But the market was changing; instead of merely supplying a need, manufacturers were having to contend with desires.

Edward Baines noted this development in Yorkshire Past and Present.

"For the first 30 years of this century the woollen manufacturer was confined almost together to plain clothes and cassimeres generally in self colours, with a few grey mixtures. About 1830 what are called fancy trowserings came into fashion. At first they were of very sober colouring, and merely a bold twill for pattern. In a very few years, however, the variety of design and colouring became much greater...

"For a long time the Northern manufacturers confined themselves to rapidity and extent of production, neglecting the essential art of design. They were consequently greatly distanced by other districts and countries (France for Cashmere), where the inhabitants were wiser in their generation. Their materials and combinations were good, but the taste which was needful to make them compete in their attractiveness with the productions of rival looms was absent. The remedy soon followed the perception of the defect. Schools of design were established about 20 years ago."

Ruskin was not interested in the fads and fancies of fashion; but he did apply his high-minded precepts to the practical problems facing his audience of textile manufacturers and artisans. The solution lay in opening men's eyes to the natural beauty of God's creation.

This is part of his 1859 speech:-

"Without observation and experience, no design - and all the lecturings and teachings, and prizes, and principles of art, in the world are of no use, so long as you don't surround your men with happy influences and beautiful things. It is impossible for them to have the right ideas about colour, unless they see the lovely colours of nature unspoiled; impossible for them to supply beautiful incident and action in their ornament, unless they see beautiful incident and action in the world about them.

Inform their minds, refine their habits, and you form and refine their designs; but keep them illiterate, uncomfortable and in the midst of beautiful things, and what ever they do will still be spurious, vulgar and valueless."

He believed that beauty ennobled the spirit, nourishing all that was good and capable of improvement.

The Bradford in which the passionate Ruskin shook his ginger whiskers had barely begun to tackle the physical depredations wrought on its panoramic landscape. Daily the senses of people were assailed by the racket and stink of unregulated money-making. And yet Bradford was surrounded by the heart-stopping beauty of the countryside and the majesty of the Dales. It still is.

Manufacturers of cloth forgot that the cloth market encompassed the non-industrial parts of society too. The well-to-do wanted variety, splendour, something expensive, fitting to their new social station.

Dyeing, however, was an art which Bradford did not begin to learn until Edward Ripley moved from Halifax to set up a dye house in Bowling. Edward Baines, writing in about 1870, noted:-

"For a long time dyers experienced great difficulty in imparting variety of colour to worsted stuffs ...The mordant or base of preparation for dyeing most in use until about 30 years ago, was copperas; but about 1839 or 1840 bi-chromate of potash was introduced; and its adoption completely revolutionised the trade, not only because it largely increased the number of colours obtainable, but because of the greater rapidity of its action. Before the use of bi-chrome a black dyed piece took a day to prepare and another to dye; the whole process can now be accomplished in two hours."

After Europe's revolutionary upheavals of 1848 (Richard Wagner on the barricades in Dresden), France's Second Empire exploded with fashions in which "overwhelming violets, cruel pinks, glaring greens and blinding yellows" became the norm for wealthy ladies, colours which were seen only in three kinds of light: daylight, firelight and gaslight.

From 1880, when electricity started to replace gas as the main source of nocturnal illumination, colours were literally seen in another kind of light. Electricity does not lend itself to the chiaroscuro effects of firelight and gaslight. Colours no longer needed to shriek to make a statement.

The use of colour, pattern and design in textile manufacture and fashion leads directly to instruction in the visual arts.

Compulsory elementary education was still nearly 20 years away when Ruskin lectured Bradford's artisans on the need to be surrounded by beautiful colours. But the town had at least four institutions concerned with art: the Bradford School of Art, the Mechanics' Institute School of Art, the Bradford Art Society, and the Church of England School of Art.

In 1878 the Technical College was founded. Debts of £14,000 which had been accumulated by 1899 saw the college pass into the hands of Bradford Corporation, whose first act was to abolish design courses. Eventually, the city's various art schools combined and became the very art college at which David Hockney spent four years drawing for up to 12 hours a day.

In the random developments which led to the formation of Bradford Art College it is tempting to see the hand of fate, shaping events like an artist's pencil. That was the institution where David Hockney was to learn his craft as an artist.

The young Titus Salt, whose chief delight at school was drawing, was also an artist at heart. His schoolmaster, Mr Harrison, declared that he was "never a bright pupil" but went on to extol the youngster's "eye". The same could be said of Mr Davies, David Hockney's form master.

The Bradford Grammar School report card which the 16-year-old Hockney took home in July 1953 showed that, like Salt, he was considered "never very bright". Of eight subjects listed he came fifth in divinity, fourth in history, and first in art.

Mr Davies noted that he showed especial proficiency in cartoon drawing and sign writing. "Although fundamentally a serious-minded boy, he has allowed his form-mates from his Third Form days to make him an almost legendary figure of fun."

The third maverick who has played such a vital role in the fortunes of Salts Mill, Jonathan Silver, went to Bradford Grammar School too. Like Hockney he didn't care for the regime of learning which conflicted with his own creative instincts. Had he devoted as much energy to learning Latin as he put into bunking off school to attend auctions he might have turned out to be yet another merely adequate scholar. Fortunately, he followed his instincts.

Creative people, whether artists or engineers, always rise above the estimation of their teachers.

Had John Ruskin returned to life during the 1980s and early 1990s, a period when the rich got immeasurably richer and surplus wealth was something to flaunt, he might have been less disparaging about Salt's motives. Although Salt was never a Socialist, his concern for the well-being of others was genuine, for he believed that in another life he would be held to account for his actions. He spent so much money making his vision a reality that within 20 years of his death the firm at Saltaire went bankrupt.

7. DECLINE AND FALL

The last day of June, 1968, was a sweltering Sunday. Paul McCartney, the Beatles' singer-songwriter and bass guitarist, spent the day in Saltaire conducting the Black Dyke Mills brass band in a recording of his tune Thingumebob. Yellow Submarine was on the flip side. The following day submarine would have been the best mode of transport in Bradford. A torrential storm of oriental proportions plunged the city centre under several feet of water in minutes.

Salts Mill was still a going concern in 1968. Within 17 years, however, it was closed and seemed doomed to end its days as a crumbling monument to the past. It had been part of Titus Salt's dynastic empire for only 38 years.

In 1892 the great enterprise foundered on the rocks of bankruptcy only 15 years after Salt's death. The Bradford Antiquary of 1987 lists three principal reasons why this happened:-

Firstly, mixed fancy goods for which Bradford was pre-eminent went out of fashion after 1876. Secondly, there was greater competition in worsteds from overseas whose home markets were protected by high tariffs, particularly the United States. Thirdly, Salt's sons were not as committed to the "works" and the community of Saltaire.

Salt's will had provided handsomely for his family, leaving Sir William Henry Salt and Herbert £100,000 each and £80,000 to each of his three daughters. Financial independence was good for them, but not for the mill.

The son who might have maintained the empire and sustained the dynasty, Titus Junior, died at the age of 44.

According to The Bradford Antiquary: "They were a different breed from Sir Titus Salt and the self-made men of his generation. The Salt family represented an extreme example of this process of withdrawal from the business community to which they owed their prosperity. Indeed, by 1892, only one of the five sons, Edward, remained as an active member of the firm. Of the others, Titus had died in 1887; George was living comfortably in London; Herbert had been a gentleman farmer for many years; and William Henry has retired to the life of a country gentleman in Leicestershire." In July 1881 the firm was registered as a limited liability company under the directorships of Edward Salt, Titus Salt Junior, Charles Stead and William Stead. But bad times were just around the corner.

Our guide to the years from the 1880s to 1958 is Donald Hanson, whose booklet, Salts Mill and Museum, was researched by J. Stanley King who worked at the mill from 1953 to 1985.

"The American market which had hitherto proved so profitable was effectively closed to imports of plush fabric in 1890 when President McKinley imposed heavy duties on manufactured products. In an effort to continue the trade, Salts established a plush fabric plant at Bridgeport, USA, but the venture was a failure."   Profits fell and the workforce was cut from 4,000 to 3,000. Sir Titus Salt, Baronet, Sons and Company Ltd. was wound up in September, 1892. It was taken over the following June by a syndicate of four Bradford businessmen: John Rhodes, John Maddocks, Isaac Smith and James Roberts.

Roberts, born in Haworth in 1848, became the sole owner in 1899 after the retirement of the other three. He disposed of his assets in February 1918, and a second syndicate consisting of Sir James Hill and his sons Arthur and Albert, Henry Whitehead and Ernest Gates, paid £2 million for the mill and the village. The company was reorganised six years later.

"The post-war boom ensured that its world famous mohair was in great demand for car upholstery, and its alpaca for golfing jackets and imitation skin coats. Raw materials from South Africa, South America, Australia, India and China still finished their long journey to the mill by canal barge, as coal was delivered by rail and canal," says Donald Hanson.

Britain's withdrawal from the Gold Standard in 1931 acted as a stimulus to the textile trade. By August 1933 Salts was busier than it had been for years, and by November production had doubled in 12 months.

Hanson lists the multiplicity of fabrics manufactured at the mill in 1937: mohair, alpaca, cashmere, camel hair, crossbred and botany yarns for both men and women's clothing, serges or fancy worsted and mohair suitings for men's wear in great variety, including Belwarp - fabrics guaranteed to be proof against both sun and sea. For women there were serges, gabardines, plain and fancy costume cloths and dress goods, as well as mohair and alpaca linings. Then war was declared.

"Throughout the war the looms disgorged countless miles of khaki, navy blue and air force blue fabrics. The welfare department was enlarged to cater for the influx of displaced persons (Eastern Europeans); the canteens were extended and modernised for Italian female operatives whose native habit of nude bathing in the canal endeared them to the youth of Saltaire."

In 1954 J.B. Priestley recalled the dirty grandeur of the industrial Bradford of his youth, when muck and brass had co-existed.

"I remember as a boy in Bradford there were enormous differences in money matters - one man might be a millionaire and another getting his thirty shillings a week, but they still called each other 'Sam' and 'Joe', and there was no nonsense between them. And the men who made the money out of the muck lived with it, which was a very good thing in our view. You knew where he lived - not far from the mill - and if you disliked him you could always throw a brick through his window. There's a lot to be said for that." Other changes occurred too. The principal one was to the workforce in the mills. Pakistani Muslims began to arrive in the mid-to-late 1950s. The men came to work the nightshift in the mills which British women were not allowed to do by law. Foreign competition had obliged mill owners to keep their factories working all through the night. They found a pool of compliant and cheap labour in the Mirpur region.

Like the Sikhs who had preceded them, the Pakistani workers saw the post-war cities of Britain's industrial North as an opportunity in which to raise some capital and improve their lot. Though many were remunerated at half the rate of the average indigenous manual worker the wage was still more than they could expect in their own country.

In the late 1950s Hindus from the Gujarat and Punjab arrived and began to settle in the north of Bradford. From their ranks came doctors, teachers, and corner-shop owners.

All these different peoples brought with them new names, new sounds, new habits, new festivals, and new ways of doing things. Bradfordians, used to assimilating and accommodating Europeans, had to learn that Singhs were Sikhs, Patels were Hindus, and Mohammads and Alis were Muslims.

Illingworth Morris & Company plc acquired Salts (Saltaire) Ltd. in 1958 for £4,740,000. Fourteen years later Woolcombers Ltd. was added to the group and all combing activity was transferred from Salts to Bradford.

J. Stanley King, a genial, Victorian-bearded man and a Bradford councillor for 25 years, recalls that the company was broken up into three sectors.

Combing was taken away to Woolcombers Ltd., which left a good deal of the mill empty. The dyeing sector was closed down altogether. Spinning was put under the control of Daniel Illingworth Ltd. The overheads fell on the remaining weaving sector.

With the changes in the wool trade many traditional markets disappeared - Canada, Cyprus, the USSR, and a big market in the Middle East. King says the 1979 Iranian revolution lost the firm a tremendous section of the trade. In later years Salts relied on trade with Kuwait.

Illingworth Morris, which had nearly been bought out by Salts in 1958, was asked to consider a management buy-out. Stanley King said they agreed. Salts got backing from the bankers and Illingworth Morris. Then Stroud Riley Drummond came along, rival competitors for the Kuwaiti trade, and made an offer which Illingworth Morris accepted.

Stroud Riley Drummond later closed Salts. A great shame for the likes of Stanley King for whom the mill was: "A lovely place to work. When I started there trade was phenomenal. The directors sat down on Friday afternoons and would buy several

Opposite: Built to last: Salt's stone houses and cobbled street from Albert Terrace, inviting you to walk around.
Photo: Economic Development Unit

Between the railway (right) and the Leeds-Liverpool canal (dividing the two mills): Salts c1950. The village spans either side of Victoria Road.   *Photo: Wood Visual Communications*

million pounds-worth of combed wool. There was no worry about the bank rate.

"We used to buy from South Africa, Australia, Montevideo. We had our own wool buyers out in Australia. It was very stimulating to see such big things going on; we had firms all over the place.

"I set up the Salts Museum in one of the former combing cellars in 1982. We had the original pattern books from 1853, including some material exhibited at Crystal Palace in 1851. There were photographs and plans. When Salts was closed the museum was given to Bradford Archives and partly to the Industrial Museum."   Up until 1975 Illingworth Morris was run by Isidore and Maurice Ostrer. When they died the controlling interest of the Ostrer estates in the company passed to Mrs Pamela Mason, the daughter of Isidore and the ex-wife of the Huddersfield-born movie star James Mason. Her 53 per cent holding led to a seat on the board in 1976 and a power struggle.

"Do I remember the Pamela Mason saga? You bet I do!" Stanley King replied in response to my question. "It provided many months of amusement, amazement, speculation and irritation for the staff and workforce, though probably not for the directors concerned."

He remembers the late Mrs Mason, who made a cameo appearance in Woody Allen's film comedy Everything You Wanted To Know About Sex But Were Too Afraid to Ask, as short and squat, an unsmiling figure in black who saw the mill as a hotbed of perpetual industrial unrest. The last strike had occurred in May, 1926.

"It was widely believed that there were only two features of Salts Mill of which she approved - the Jubilee Room (a former counting house expensively refurbished for a visit by Princess Anne in 1977, the Queen's Jubilee Year, and from which the staff were disdainfully barred), and the office cat. When, therefore, the former was befouled by the latter, the mill was filled with surreptitious merriment," he said.

To celebrate this fine mess, Stanley penned an appropriate poem which, to his alarm, reached the highest echelons of the firm - but not the cat-loving Mrs Mason. Eventually she tired of boardroom battles and in 1981 sold her shares. She retreated with her millions and her cats to the luxury of her Beverly Hills estate on Pamela Drive. She died in 1996.

In 1970, approximately 1,142,000 people in the UK were employed in textiles and clothing. By 1991 and the second recession in ten years (said to be the worst since the 1930s), that figure had shrunk to just 347,000.

West Yorkshire once had scores of thousands of textile workers, many of them highly skilled who operated sophisticated machinery. In 1991, however, there were just 45,000, of which 12,681 worked in the Bradford Metropolitan District.

Peter Booth, National Secretary of the Transport & General Workers Union textile trade group, based in Bradford, has worked for more than 30 years on the shop floor and as a full-time union official.

He attributes the decline to new imported looms as well as weaving, dyeing and finishing machinery coming in from abroad - machinery which used to be made in the UK. Competition from Hong Kong, China and Taiwan - manufacturing clothing behind high tariff barriers and heavily subsidised by government - also hit the home market, as did competition from low-cost Italian wool fabrics.

In the 1980s an over-valued currency, high interest rates and high inflation combined to make life even more difficult. Businesses went bust or, as in the case of Salts, were purchased by rivals and closed down.

"In the past factories would lay off workers, but now you have two bad quarters and you're looking down the barrel of a gun. Nowadays if you're down you're out. It's the financial system; everybody wants a return.

"In the past firms had bad periods, but kept the looms and the mills. Large companies with resources, family firms, have survived; but those who have to go to the banks haven't.

"Twenty years ago companies would expect to have their bad times and would stick it out. That's changed in the past 15 years. Everything is short term the way things are financially structured now - by accountants, people without a wider knowledge of what the industry is about. Textiles is a basic manufacturing industry that has to look to the medium and long term - two to ten years.

"More money is made than earned these days. In Salt's day people made money by making things".

Micro-technology, now thriving at Salts Mill, has less than 20 years of tradition in a city where the staple industry for the best part of 150 years employed thousands. The closure of Salts Mill in February 1986 symbolised the end of a tradition. In October 1996 Bradford's Telegraph & Argus published a review of the district's leading 50 companies. Not a single textile firm was in the first 25. The top ten were concerned with food and distribution, chemicals, financial services, mail order, and stationery. Pace Micro Technology plc, in 15th spot, had moved up six places on the previous year.

Titus Salt's empire, which had once spanned the world, was emptied of machinery and left to look after itself. The yards which had echoed to the sound of thousands of people hurrying to and from their work were silent, the decks of windows unlit from within. Like a great stone ship the mill was abandoned; the roof alone required repairs estimated at £150,000.

Amid the inevitable rows about job losses, there was talk about what to do with the buildings which, as far as Illingworth Morris was concerned, were unwanted. One idea was to turn Salts into a transport museum.

On April 27, 1987 the Telegraph & Argus announced news of a report compiled by consultants KMG Thomson McLintock. The report set out how the mill could be redeveloped into an industrial and leisure complex at a cost of £14.5 million. Although the 112-page document had been completed that February, Bradford Council had not got round to discussing its contents.

Former English teacher Clive Woods, long-serving chairman of Saltaire Village Society, accused the council of leaving the mill to rot along with Saltaire's other public buildings. The council pointed out, quite rightly, that it did not own the building. To all intents and purposes the mill was dead, a monolithic relic of the age of heroic materialism.

"It was the era of Brunel, of people who did things that nobody had conceived", said Stanley King. Resurrecting the place seemed about as likely as raising the Titanic from the bottom of the North Atlantic.

8. THE RISE OF SALTS

Like all showmen, Jonathan Silver loves surprising people - especially those who have known him for a long time. One of David Hockney's brothers, Paul, a chartered accountant, former Liberal councillor and Lord Mayor of Bradford, has known Silver for many years.

"He used to ring up and say, 'Guess what I've done? Go on, have a guess.' I'd say, 'I don't know Jonathan.' That didn't stop him though. Well, one day he rang and said to me, ' You'll never guess what I've just done.' I said, 'You're right, I can't. 'He said, 'I've just bought Salts Mill.' " Silver and his family had returned from travelling round the world. It was May 1987, and the country was preparing for a General Election. He wasn't sure that he wanted to remain in England, although he was both intrigued and excited by the prospective sale of the mill. Unable to sit and wait for something to turn up, he busied himself with his favourite occupation: looking for an opportunity.

Before long he was driving down Victoria Road to inspect the premises at the bottom of the hill.

Clive Woods runs a second-hand book shop a stone's throw from the mill. With his bald forehead, florid cheeks and beard, he looks like a pocket Cèzanne. His eyes blaze behind his black framed glasses when he remembers the state of the village at that time.

"Saltaire was abandoned and forgotten. The Department of Transport wanted to put four lanes of highway through the village via the park. The local authority and the county council didn't seem to be bothered. Locals fought that one off and won the argument.

"At that point we had one derelict mill on one side of the canal and an empty mill, Salts, on the other side. Victoria Hall was shut because it was in a dangerous state and the school was closed for the same reason. The whole area looked as if it was going to disintegrate," he said.

Illingworth Morris had sold off the various parts of the textile operation, but had retained the ownership of the mill. Silver opened what he calls "a dialogue"; but the inconclusiveness of the exercise wearied him. Erroneously, as things turned out, he was convinced Illingworth Morris did not really want to sell.

On the very evening of the General Election, he had his first and only conversation, on the telephone, with Alan Lewis, chairman and chief executive of the company. It was short and strange, he said, as if Lewis was selling something with which he didn't know what to do.

Lewis says he was keen to get rid of the building, to the right buyer. He had offered it to Bradford Council with a 25-year lease. The Council didn't want it. Silver says the importance of Saltaire, the threat of demolition, had attracted the attention of the Press. He suspects there were other prospective purchasers too.

"Although it was a 17-acre site mill it wasn't worth much: Illingworth Morris just couldn't see this. The only moment regeneration can take place to an area like Saltaire is when the owners accept that what they think is worth a great deal of money actually isn't. That moment came to Alan Lewis on the evening of June 10th, 1987. He said to me, 'You'll make a fortune out of it.' I said to him, 'That's what I intend to do.' Otherwise what was the point in me buying it?" Silver formed a company, Salts Estates Ltd., to buy the mill; he was to be the sole owner. He paid some of the money personally and raised the rest from Barclays. He won't say how much the mill cost him; most people assume the price for such a large site must have been in the region of £1 million. Lewis maintains that Illingworth Morris sold it for a very low price.

Silver also negotiated for some of the objects the firm had left behind, principally the splendid blue and gold watercolour of the spinning mill. He bought it personally, and had the sense to use it as the design for Salts Estates' official letter-head.

Alan South, Jonathan's close friend since their days at Bradford Grammar School, had left Dean Clough to become Project Manager at Salts. He confirms that Alan Lewis insisted Jonathan's offer be made under Personal Seal, which makes the purchaser personally liable.

"The exchange of contracts took place on June 10th with completion on July 10th. In between Jonathan and I were not allowed into the mill. We could only take people round by asking for the keys from the security man in the gatehouse. So we just sat in the car outside for a month with a mobile phone and got coffee brought down to us from the village."

Shortly after Silver became the mill's fifth owner, Prince Charles's then-architectural adviser Rod Hackney arrived to offer his not inexpensive services.

Anybody turning up on the doorstep looking for business was to be admired as far as Silver was concerned, so he hired him. Reports of explosive rows soon reached the ears of Silver's former colleagues at Dean Clough. All he will say about this episode is that Hackney's services cost him in the region of £60,000 in return for which he got one very good piece of advice: not to be in a hurry to let space.

The idea of an exclusively David Hockney gallery was put in Silver's mind during a brief run of performances by the IOU Theatre Company at the mill as part of the first Bradford Festival. He ran a bar for the duration, in the course of which he says he suddenly thought the spinning mill would make a striking art gallery.

The following morning he set about turning the idea into reality. South said the project released Silver's considerable locked-up energy.

"His modus operandi in tackling a building is at complete variance with any established practice, and above all he just gets stuck in. That can be very irritating, and contributed to more of our arguments than anything else.

Setting a good example: Jonathan Silver (right) surveys progress in restoring Salt's original stone setts in 1988. *Photo: Jonathan Silver*

"I am relatively unconventional, but I have a very conventional mind in the way that it works. Jonathan can be conventional in some ways, but his mind is totally unconventional. That's why architects and engineers, people who love to sit in meetings and plan things on paper, don't get on with him. I don't think he has any time for professions except doctors. He's only interested in people who do things. The more they do the more interested he is in them. Jonathan is not a dreamer - he acts."

South is right. Take the following example. In 1979 Silver reacted to John Pilger's film about Pol Pot's Kampuchea, The Year Zero, by suddenly flying out to that ruined country with Michael Hickling, a young Yorkshire Post reporter. Silver's parents, Sydney and Irene, were in Japan when they got a call from Silver's wife Maggie. "You'd better sit down before I tell you, your son has gone off to Cambodia to do some reporting," she told them. Irene later told me: "He took some incredible photographs which he sold to the National Geographic. They bought the photos for quite a lot of money which he sent to UNICEF. There are a lot of people with consciences in the world, but it takes a bit of doing to get up and go."

Not long after buying Salts, Silver employed a team of men to strip the tarmac from the front of the building and restore the original stone sets which Sir Titus had laid in

1852-53.

Unable to watch them having all the fun, he insisted on having a go on a pneumatic drill. He was having the time of his life when the branch director of Barclays Bank arrived with other bank officials. John Clapham was so startled by the sight of the bejeaned owner of Salts Mill jumping up and down with a road drill that he dined out on the story ever after.

The spinning mill that was to house the 1853 Hockney Gallery needed an immense amount of renovation. Silver launched himself at the task with his customary zeal. A more cautious soul might have contemplated the proposition for a while, got things down on paper. But once Silver had made up his mind to make the world's most famous living artist the "patron saint of Salts Mill", to quote the journalist Michael Church, he could not contain himself .

How the 1853 Hockney Gallery used to look. Jonathan Silver (left) and former assistant Alan South carry a Hockney across the muck. *Photo: Telegraph & Argus*

9. SILENCE IS GOLDEN, SILVER IS NOT

"You become rich the moment you have something that somebody else wants," Jonathan Silver once told me, repeating one of David Hockney's observations. Silver appears to have known this from a very early age. When he was ten he bought up job lots of lost pens, pencils and erasers and sold them back to his fellow pupils. At the age of 12 he told his parents not to give him any more pocket money: in future he would provide his own. For the last 35 years he has usually been in the position of having something somebody else wanted.

He was born in October 1949 (100 years after Salt had conceived of his plan to build the mill), at 4 Clifton Villas. Irene's mother Gertrude Morris ran the place as a boarding house for Jewish refugees. One of the guests who lived there for about six years was Benjamin Kagan, father of the Gannex coat manufacturer Lord (Joe) Kagan. Two years later in 1951, Silver's brother Robin was born there.

Irene first met Sydney Silver in 1946 when he called at the house to look up her brother Sidney, whom he had met during a ten-year sojourn in Palestine. "There was this stick of liquorice, black as the ace of spades, in a long coat and a black hat, and I thought 'Yuck!'" Irene said.

She had been born in Peel Square, at the top end of Bradford's Lumb Lane. In 1926 it was "very elegant and posh", she said, playfully extentuating the vowel in "posh". Educated at Grange Girls' High School and a domestic science college in Leeds, she was a school meals supervisor when she opened the front door that fateful day in 1946 and first caught sight of her future husband.

Sydney Silver was born during a Zeppelin raid on Hull in 1917. His parents, Nathan and Rebecca, both died from heart disease before he was 11 years old. Sydney and his younger brother Bobby were sent to boarding school in Brussels. Later he went to Palestine. He was a Zionist. Despite his unpromising appearance on the doorstep of 4 Clifton Villas, Irene fell in love and they were married on New Year's Day, 1947.

For nine years he made a living as a market trader in Keswick, Kendal and Wakefield. But as a university-educated man, capable of thinking and conversing in several languages, he wanted something better for himself and his family. For a time he had joint ownership of a haberdashery shop in Bingley. Then he bought a burling and mending business (repairing cloth) at 17a Barry Street in central Bradford. That was in 1958. The following year he opened the first of his three Wimpy Bars in

What poise, what self-assurance, what style (note the button-down trouser pockets): Jonathan Silver the boy showing all the confidence of a precocious violin virtuoso. *Photo: Jonathan Silver*

Broadway (the other two were in Halifax and Leeds). It was in the Bradford fast food diner that Jonathan was to have his first meeting with a rather important local artist in the summer of 1963.

Sydney sold the Wimpy Bars to Grand Metropolitan in 1972. Eight years later he also sold his mohair suit manufacturing business, Atomic Mohair, to Stroud Riley Drummond - the very firm which was to close Salts Mill. 1980 was also the year that Sydney was obliged to undergo open heart surgery, which was not so commonplace then as it is now. The operation was successful. He and Irene decided the time had come to move to a warmer climate. They spent the next ten years in Marbella, where Sydney acquired yet another language and used the arm which had made him a champion fencer at university to paint landscapes. In 1990, three years after Jonathan had bought Salts Mill, they returned to England to be closer to their sons and grand-daughters.

As a boy Jonathan had "ants in his pants", Irene says. When he was 11 she took him to his first concert at St George's Hall to hear the Halle Orchestra. After ten minutes she had to leave because her fidgety son had been unable to sit still during the performance. He still has a low boredom threshold. Music did not mean much to him then. He was more interested in animals and birds and creepy-crawly creatures which kept escaping from tanks at home. Robin says his brother was a founder member of the British Naturalist Society. Jonathan retains his childhood passion for cats. At the age of 46 he added a dachshund to the menagerie of animals at home. The dog's name is Frieda, perhaps after D. H. Lawrence's wife.

Sydney and Irene Silver decided that Bradford Grammar School was the best place for their boys. It was a direct grant school in those days, private but inexpensive.

Jonathan passed the entrance examination and became an unwilling pupil, firstly at the junior grammar in Manningham Lane, and then at the senior school in Keighley Road. He hated school.

"I was always in the G Stream, the bottom stream, and was always bottom of the class. I never did well. I disliked the way everything was taught: no emphasis on learning to learn, no scope for talking or dialogue - just listening. One report said I was scatter-brained and would not get on. Another said: Silence is golden, Silver is not. I just felt it was a terrible waste of time." Entering the classroom one morning he saw on the blackboard a target, like an archery target, with an arrow in it and 'Death to all yids' written across the top of the blackboard.

When the teacher started the lesson as though nothing had happened, Silver remonstrated with him. His response struck the boy as non-committal, so he walked out and went to see the deputy head Mr. Twelves. Silver said he never spoke to the teacher again.

There were few Jewish boys in the school, maybe 18 or 20 out of about 1,000. He was 15 or so and says he was, at that time, trying to make sense of the Holocaust.

Robin Silver acknowledges that anti-Semitism was a tangible part of the school's ambience. So does Alan South. He first met Jonathan at the school and says anti-Semitism was a feature of life in 1960s Bradford and should not be under-estimated.

"If you were the sort of Jewish person who conformed, was good at games or was straight forwardly clever, that was okay; but if you were different it was attributed to your being Jewish.

"I noticed Jonathan's capacity to exclude other things or people and concentrate on things that mattered to him. A lot of talented people I have met are the same: that's how they concentrate. At an early age at school Jonathan would come across like that; if nobody had anything to say to him that mattered he would just ignore them. He didn't have an adult's capacity to mask that which, of course, he has now. I don't think he ever felt himself superior to other people as a general rule.

"Jonathan has little patience with hierarchies of any description, he has no respect for them. It's his approach to business. If he went into a bank and saw the managing director behind the counter he would find that perfectly normal, it might even increase his respect." Playwright and actor Alan Bennett remembers that in post-war Leeds there was a good deal of anti-Semitism.

"I can remember Jewish boys in my school being regularly bullied, one boy in particular, Alan Harris, always coming in for it. The masters used to turn a blind eye and even collaborating, one master catching him a terrific slap across the face for very little reason," he recalls in his TV programme about Leeds City Art Gallery, Portrait or Bust.

Bottom of the class, the target of racist abuse: no wonder the young Silver felt at odds with school and was attracted to out-and-out rebels like Alan South.

South was a member of the ANARCHS, a mischief-making group of four boys whose anti-establishment exploits included dyeing the school swimming pool purple before a big gala, and hiding a large David Hockney painting (A view of Bradford from Earls Court) in the monitors' common room. The school authorities feigned indifference which, naturally enough, infuriated Alan and his chums. They painted a large red question mark in the place where A View of Bradford From Earls Court had been hanging. Again, there was no reaction. In the end the ANARCHS put the picture back.

Silver liked Alan's free spirit, his anarchic sense of fun, his attitude to life, and particularly his liberality. South was drawn to Silver for two reasons: he was different from everybody else and liked Alan who, in turn, was delighted by Silver's tendency to ask outrageous questions in class.

"In the middle of a geology lesson the teacher was explaining how nobody believed the biblical explanation of the Creation any more, that Adam and Eve had been replaced by Darwin's Theory of Evolution. He couldn't get any further because this voice kept saying, 'Sir, sir, sir, I believe in Adam and Eve sir: one man, one woman - seems logical to me'. So the teacher said, 'Well everybody accepts Darwin these days - except Silver'.

"Another time a teacher was going on about not standing about with your hands in your pockets. Jonathan interrupted him saying, 'Sir, I don't stand around with my hands in my pockets. I don't have any pockets. I get my mother to sew them up, because pockets spoil the line of the trousers'."

As far as Silver was concerned the only good thing about school was the extended lunch break, which lasted from 12.25pm to 2pm.

"I was on the 12.26pm trolley bus every day into Bradford, which took about four minutes, digested a Wimpy and chips at the Wimpy Bar my father had opened in Broadway, and by 12.45pm I was in John H. Raby's auction room, or De Rome's.

"If anyone wants a lesson in buying and selling they should go to an auction room. I spent years in auction rooms, understanding the value of junk and learning what was an antique. Those were the days when real antiques were coming out of houses in Bradford; I just learned by watching the dealers buying antiques and junk. You could predict what they would pay. Two days a week I would go to the reference library to look at books about antiques.

"By the time I was 14 or 15 maybe, I was buying and selling in Raby's at lunch times. I just found it terribly entertaining. I used to have an account there. You could buy an 18th Century gate-leg table for a few pounds. It was possible to make between £5 and £10 a week, which was a lot of money in those days."

The teenage tycoon also had an egg round which he started with a friend, Derek Peers, who went to Belle Vue Boys' School.

Most youngsters were content to earn pocket-money for the pictures, confectionery, the odd cigarette, by delivering newspapers or working in a shop or on a Saturday market stall. At the age of 13, Silver knew the value of working for oneself, providing a legitimate gap in the market could be found and supplied.

He recalls that the idea of selling eggs came to him when the Egg Marketing Board was created to fix the price of eggs and standardise them by means of a little red lion. From listening to friends' parents and relatives, he discovered that there was a demand for fresh eggs.

A farmer agreed to sell Silver and his partner 100-dozen eggs a week for cash. They carted them round the better roads and avenues of Shipley and Frizinghall, selling a dozen eggs for five shillings (25p) - undercutting the market by threepence or sixpence.

He was the eggman for three years. The experience taught him a valuable business lesson: the customer, even a quirky one, is always right.

When he wasn't delivering eggs, he was becoming increasingly intrigued by the 'articles for sale' and 'articles wanted' columns in the Telegraph & Argus newspaper, noticing that the same dealers names kept recurring.

He rang up a woman who regularly offered things for sale, and realised that what she was selling - Hoover Juniors - had been acquired at auctions. He knew enough about buying and selling to work out that the difference in the mark-up between selling by auction and selling through an advert was about double.

In those days treasures were still being sold. Because Bradford had been at the heart of the Industrial Revolution and so much wealth had been created in a short time, the quality of the best objects was very high.

"The wealth of Bradford was based on textiles and that in turn had created wonderful Victorian villas and mills like Lister's and Salts. It was uncanny watching the antiques being sold off - anticipating the desecration of Bradford's architectural heritage which supposedly no one wanted anymore. It was a coincidence that these objects made their way into sales rooms when I was at Bradford Grammar. People didn't know what antiques were worth because there were no catalogues; the market was still being created."

Silver, attuned to the value of both junk and antiques, was also aware of the burgeoning market for them in Portobello Road and other parts of Swinging London, when Harold Wilson's Labour Government was in power.

Jack Hook, a fireman until he was 50, and a friend of the Silver family for more than 40 years, remembers Silver's early passion for what he insisted on calling antiques. Jack had a blue Commer Van which Silver used for delivering cloth and objets d'art.

Silver had accumulated a pile of stuff from houses in Shipley that were being demolished (access to the site was gained by presenting the foreman with three-and-a-half yards of suit cloth). Jack considered the most appropriate destination for the assorted objects was the nearest rubbish dump. Silver took them to London, sold the lot in half-an-hour for a good profit. When he came back he smiled and said: "That's as much as you know about the bloody job!" He would have been about 17.

Silver bought harmoniums, pianos, handles off the doors of the Gaumont, and a huge chandelier from the same place. Jack was the collector. Although he sometimes protested and swore blue murder, he enjoyed Silver's flair; he never knew what was going to happen next.

Jack also worked on commission for Illingworth Morris, delivering cloth. Sometimes Silver accompanied him on these trips to the mill. While waiting, he studied the building's architecture, and in time grew fond of it.

Silver persuaded a friend, Paul Barnard, to drive a van-load of 'antiques' to London which he sold to a woman in a shop in Portobello Road for about £190. The year would have been 1965, when £190 was far more than George Best's weekly wage at Manchester United. While Jonathan was in London he took the opportunity to run his eye over men's fashions in trendy Carnaby Street and later Chelsea's Kings Road. An idea was germinating in his hyper-active mind, an idea that wouldn't come to fruition until he had left school and completed a three-year-degree course at Leeds University in the summer of 1971.

The G-stream dunce seriously applied himself to his studies from the age of 15. He had reconciled himself to gaining the necessary qualifications that would serve as his passport out of school. He took four GCE A Levels in Economics, History, British Constitution and Politics (this subject he took at Bradford College), but without the offer of an interview from any of the six universities he had nominated on his UCCA form.

e gloves came on, who had the upper.
s Buffini's sensational comedy looks
losed doors of the palace to speculate
appened when two of the most
in the world clashed.

nsightful and brilliantly sharp satire
ted for an Olivier Award for Best
ly in 2015 and went on to be a
nash hit.

17687 74411 Online: theatrebythelake.com

e John Thorpe.

Callan x2

y Strickett.
ne & Sabino (

"What have you got by way of Barber of Seville that's good? I don't want English singers. Give me Barber of Seville by Maria Callas". *Photo: Salts Estates*

That didn't matter then, for within a week of taking his examinations and walking away from school for the last time, he was on a Jumbo Jet to Israel - to volunteer for the army in the wake of the Six Day War.

He was convinced that the State of Israel, which was only a year or two older than he was, needed all the help it could get to defend itself against Nasser's Egypt and other border enemies. Many young Jews felt the same way in 1967.

His parents say he lied about his age, but when the Israeli military discovered that their latest recruit was only 17 they asked him to leave the tank regiment he had joined. Silver won't say much about his brief spell in uniform. Close friends say he was given the job of removing corpses from a battlefield. He says he just got fed up with sleeping rough, marching over parched terrain and getting bitten by bugs. Having ants in your pants in the desert is no fun, evidently.

Having extricated himself from the army he spent the remainder of that summer working in a semi-automatic car wash in Tel Aviv. Upon receiving the good news from home that he had passed his A Levels, he decided to return to England via Rome, where he spent a fortnight looking at paintings. He hitched the rest of the way, stopping off for a few days in Paris. As a point of principle he says he only accepted lifts from Mercedes and Ferraris.

He arrived back in Bradford and obtained from a former teacher a testimonial which secured him a place at university. But after four weeks of studying business at Enfield College of Technology, a very bored Jonathan once again returned to Bradford. He was 18 and had decided to become an artist.

"I had the upstairs room above my father's textile business in Barry Street. That year I became a painter, standing on ladders and pouring paint on to canvases - non-representational abstracts - while working at the Wimpy Bar washing up, and waiting on."

The studio was also a good place for parties and for people to hang out. Robin, a founder member of the West Riding Youth Theatre, was still at Bradford Grammar School. The early meetings of the theatrical group, as well as auditions, were held in Jonathan's studio.

One Thursday night in February in walked a certain Maggie Jackson from Leeds. Jonathan's future wife looked round the walls and said: "Who did all these terrible paintings?" They fell in love. Irene Silver remembers her son coming home to Wilmer Drive and announcing that he had met the girl he was going to marry.

Maggie was going to Manchester Art College, so he decided he had better stabilise his life. His mother said he had returned from the aftermath of the Six Day War "very unhappy". Silver says he was more self-confident but still mixed up in his mind. Meeting Maggie undoubtedly gave him a purpose.

He abandoned the notion of becoming Bradford's answer to Jackson Pollock and resolved to go to Leeds University where, he had discovered, he could do a combined degree in textile management and the history of art. Lawrence Gowing, later Sir Lawrence, was head of the fine arts course and that attracted him.

Silver says he enjoyed three good years and never missed a lecture. He parked in

Making a point about regeneration over lunch in Salts Diner.   *Photo:Telegraph & Argus*

the staff car park, his immaculate three-piece suit deceiving the attendant into mistaking him for one of the staff. Students wore hippie clothes in those days.

Perhaps the boldest thing he did was to go to Manchester in search of L.S.Lowry. He had purchased an old painting in a junk shop for ten shillings (50p), which he thought Lowry might have done. He wanted the artist, then 82 or 83, to tell him if he had indeed stumbled upon an amazing piece of good fortune.

He took a bus to Mottram-in-Longdendale, Cheshire, and eventually found the reclusive former rent collector. Lowry invited him in. The house was full of clocks set at different times.

Silver says he spent eight hours with the old man, who complained about the Inland Revenue. Lowry must have enjoyed the company of the student; but he refused to say anything about the painting.

Silver, who discarded the painting years later, had no reason to suspect that this meeting would lead him to consider and take the first steps, in 1995, of creating his own Lowry gallery.

He left university a few months before his 22nd birthday. The Beatles had broken up acrimoniously: Jimi Hendrix was dead: the Conservative party was in power (Edward Heath was looking after the shop at 10 Downing Street): British troops were trying to contain 'The Troubles' in Northern Ireland: the Vietnam War was raging: Watergate had yet to happen and President Richard Nixon was starting to think about a second term of office: Czechoslovakia, East Germany and Yugoslavia were still political entities: Brezhnev, Tito and Mao Tse-Tung were still alive - as was Picasso: David Hockney was travelling in Spain and France: George Best was still playing for Manchester United: in England at least the fashion was for men to wear their hair long and their trousers flared.

Neville Silver, a cousin, was looking for rooms in Manchester to open an opticians. He acquired a suite of offices at 2 Ridgefield near Deansgate, which had belonged to a solicitor's firm (Field-Cunningham). Having got the lease he changed his mind.

At that time Silver's father was working for a man in London who had acquired some lambs wool jackets. That's how Jonathan Silver Clothes started. Silver, who knew Manchester, ran the shop. Ownership was shared by Sydney Silver, Neville Silver, the man in London and Jonathan.

The shop opened in the summer of 1971. Located in a Victorian listed building, it was doubly remarkable for having neither a conventional front window nor planning permission for a change of use. Silver saw in his new enterprise a marketing opportunity.

"The North was a wilderness for fashion in 1971; the nearest thing we had was Austin Reed's in Leeds. In those days men's wear retailing was the thing. There were two shops in London - Jeff Kwintner's Village Gate and Sid Brent's Take Six. That was the era of the Likely Lads wearing three-piece, square-shouldered suits." Those shops were supplied by a textile-manufacturer in Pudsey called Ernest Hall.

"I was supplying the cleverest retailers in England. Kwintner owned 16 shops such

But wh
hand?
behind
what re
powerf

This fu
was no
New C
West E

Box off

Carole

Rog

Hil

Elo

as Village Gate, and Squire," said Hall, now Sir Ernest. "Frankly it was a new wave which knocked the Burtons, Colliers and Hepworths for six in the post-Beatles era. It became a young man's world. You could tell the difference between the young and the old by the style of clothes they wore.

"Kwintner was king, totally extraordinary; an uncompromising individual. The interior of the shops was beautiful; there was music; more than anything they had new styles: flared trousers, waistcoats, wide lapels. The suits were pinstripe, classical, and made of the best quality wool. In the late 1960s a three-piece suit cost just under £30. Kwintner was selling 3,000 suits a week - an incredible period."

Silver knew the hippie era was over when no one bought his orange and green trousers.

Sober black and navy-blue mohair flares sold instead. Silver worked on the CMT basis - cut, make and trim, as it's known in the trade. He wasn't buying anything from a wholesaler. The only way he could see people buying clothes from him was if they were fashionable and of good value. A shop 75 yards away was selling trousers for about £9. He calculated that he could sell the same trouser for half that and still make a profit.

"That's the strongest argument for capitalism," he said. "Price mechanism allows people to innovate. Lads in Manchester of my age had to pay £9, and here was somebody selling trousers of £4.10s I left the bottoms unfinished. We offered the Quick Silver solution - on the spot shortening."

He and Maggie got married in August 1972. Their first home was 7 St. Wilfred's Street, Calverley, between Bradford and Leeds. The house was built for a man called Brassington. It was an 'upside down' house: the bedroom was downstairs, the lounge upstairs. There were four front doors. They bought it for £9,000 or £10,000, without windows or internal fittings.

Six days a week he drove to and from Manchester, a two-hour journey each way in those days before the M62. Work was the major outlet for Silver's tremendous drive and energy. Relaxation bored him; it bores him now.

"Without a challenge," says Jack Hook, "Jonathan can be a pain in the arse."

People assume that Silver has a master plan. In fact he is more pragmatic than calculating, making things up as he goes along. Master plans presuppose a belief in Providence. As an atheist he believes you make your own luck. The difference between Silver and someone else might simply come down to this: when he spots an opportunity he goes for it with all his might.

Before the decade was out there were clothes shops in Manchester, Birmingham, Coventry, Liverpool, Warrington, Sheffield, Leeds and Bradford - 13 in all. The Bradford shop, situated at the bottom of Sunbridge Road, opened in the mid-1970s. Silver had bought out his partners for what he coyly describes as "many thousands of pounds". Turnover was between one and two million pounds.

The business was based at 30 Chapel Street, Bradford, in which Silver had what Jack Hook described as an unbelievable office - telephones hanging from the ceiling, a real expresso machine in the corner. There was a clothing factory too called Noble Crest.

As his clothing empire expanded, Silver needed to find more reliable sources of cloth.

"It was mentioned to me that Leigh Mills at Stanningley, in Pudsey, was a good place. I went to see Ernest Hall and realised that we got on well from the start."

10. THE IMPORTANCE OF BEING ERNEST

On a bitterly cold and snowy Thursday night in February 1996, Sir Ernest Hall gave the annual Arts Council lecture in Dean Clough's Viaduct Theatre. He called it In Defence of Genius. Before a distinguished audience, wrapped in overcoats and scarves against the chill, Sir Ernest explained why making the arts a part of everyone's life was vital in order to secure the future of society.

The artist, he declared, was the role model for the entrepreneur that society needed - a radically different interpretation of what the word entrepreneur had come to mean in the Thatcherite 'Loadsamoney' Britain of the mid-1980s. He illuminated his text with an unforgettable image.

"I realised that the process of designing fabrics and running a business was a creative process similar to composing music or writing poetry and satisfyingly productive. The two roles seemed to fuse and I sometimes dreamt of weaving sheds at night always dramatically lit, but full of grand pianos and not weaving looms."

Ernest Hall was born in Bolton in 1930, the eldest of three boys. He attended different junior schools until the age of 11 when he won a

Friend, mentor, musician and millionaire: Sir Ernest Hall, another self-made man.
Photo: Jonathan Silver

scholarship to Bolton Municipal Secondary School. He remained there until the age of 17, when a scholarship to the Royal Manchester College of Music changed his life.

He and I first met in July, 1988, for the purpose of a newspaper interview. After nine hours in his company I was intoxicated by his energy and the enthusiasm he injected into the conversation.

"I think everybody has genius within them," he said. "If every teacher in every school treated every child as a potential genius what do you think the effect would be? If you tell somebody they can do something, give them some belief, their expectation goes up 1,000 per cent.

"Teachers without confidence in their charges are an evil influence. The qualities that are going to make you successful in life are not those you need to pass examinations. You need courage, creativity, enthusiasm. Exams might not activate these qualities. Education in the normal sense is sheer drudgery."

If Jonathan Silver heard Ernest Hall expound such views they must have been music to his ears, I know they were to mine.

"I regard myself as a secular evangelist," continued the man who had amassed a fortune as a textile magnate, travelled the world, and composed and played classical music. "We need vision in business, we need wisdom about what really matters in the long run. My main objective is to improve people's view of life."

He went into textiles after two years of National Service.

"I found textiles awe-inspiring. As a child I saw my father at work, bare-foot in the mule room - it was like a hot house - spinning very fine Egyptian cotton. When I became interested in textiles it made me see my relations in a new light. I felt a sense of warmth for those people because I understood their skills. Before that I thought they were nothing."

He looks like a cross between the actor Richard Widmark and the writer Tom Wolfe. But his hair flops across his forehead in a Russian way, and when he sits in a chair, stooping slightly as though over a keyboard, he actually gains in stature. When he stands up he seems slightly smaller and frailer.

Jonathan Silver found the older man both stimulating and amusing.

"I don't find many people stimulating, but when I do I try to cultivate friendship, just as when I met David Hockney for the first time - one of the most stimulating people I have ever met.

"I was Ernest's customer. I was spending between £50,000 and £60,000 a year with him. He was also quite generous about the way he let me tag on my orders to those of his London customers who I knew would choose the best cloth.

"He used to come to our house, after Zoë was born. He loves kids. We met his first wife, June, who was an amazingly powerful woman. I knew him through his traumas of divorce and finding his new love, Sarah. It was inevitable that one day we would end up in business together.

"He was very conscious of the success of the clothes shops; I was making a lot of money. While that was happening his company - Mountleigh - had gone public. His partner, Tony Clegg, was being a famous buccaneer. Ernest got bored with it all."

In late 1977 or early 1978, Silver and his brother Robin opened a shop in Manchester of a kind very different to the clothes emporiums.

Art and Furniture was located at 19 Chapel Walks, opposite the Royal Exchange, and sold antiques as well as prints and paintings by David Hockney and Ron Kitaj. Robin also remembers an exhibition of Bill Brandt's photographs.

The shop's chief success, however, was that it enabled the relationship with Hockney and Kitaj to develop. Art and Furniture was the precursor of things which have happened at Salts Mill since 1987, things which could not have happened otherwise.

The shop lasted about 18 months. By the time it closed the chain of Jonathan Silver Clothes shops had been sold to the John Michael empire for about £325,000. Robin says his brother always said anyone could be out of the fashion industry by the time they were thirty, and he was thirty.

"Maggie Thatcher was in power and had increased VAT from eight to thirteen per cent. I remember saying to Jonathan that it was going to be a desperate time for the retail business because no one could absorb those costs and prices were going to shoot up. It was a euphoric time in financial circles; companies wanted to buy other companies.

"John Michael had been on to us for about two years, as had others, and there was an opportunity to sell. He and I were supposed to work for John Michael in Bradford, but we got sacked after about three months.

"John Michael's owner, John Ingram, had 40 to 50 shops, mainly in the South. His shops in the North were not doing very well. I think the plan was to merge their operation with ours."

Robin spent a lot of time in London preparing a report on what was going wrong in the North. John Ingram, who liked to have others agree with him, perhaps wasn't used to dealing with people like the Silvers.

Jonathan Silver's final act as an employee was to hand over the keys of his company car, and a clutch of parking tickets. He was fairly wealthy, and in need of a new challenge, a fresh opportunity.

Ernest Hall bought fifty per cent of Art and Furniture's picture business. The day after the deal Jonathan started sharing Hall's office at Mountleigh.

The Hall-Silver partnership moved into property, buying C. & J. Hirst, an old mill in Huddersfield. The second and most significant deal occurred in 1983, the year Ernest Hall retired as Chairman and joint managing director of the Mountleigh Group, and Margaret Thatcher won her second General Election.

Silver and Hall bought Dean Clough, a former carpet factory at Halifax containing 1.25 million square feet of space. Neither of them will disclose for how much, though I believe the price was well under £1 million.

They were equal partners, each contributing 50 per cent of the cost. Silver's premonition that the partnership with the older man would be intense proved to be true. Within a year or so it was dissolved. Alan South, who had two periods of employment at Dean Clough, said the styles of these two different characters proved incompatible - in business at least.

Hall's motto at the time was: 'Procrastination is the hallmark of genius' - Hall's mark of genius. He liked to take his time before reaching a decision, the reverse of Silver's mode of operation. They have different interpretations of their time together.

"After Jonathan had had the excitement of opening Crossley's Bar, which was a great success though quite small, he decided he wanted to convert a major amount of space into a mega night club. That was a major conflict of views and I knew we couldn't work together for much longer," Sir Ernest said.

"We started off with no more complicated thought than putting in pictures which we owned (but not with a view to having a gallery), and letting space to people in business. It was extremely exciting. By the end of 1984, by the time Jonathan had left, I wanted to embrace education and all sorts of other things - the idea of a practical utopia.

"The main thing that Jonathan did when he was here was he successfully opened Crossley's Bar: that was his main thing and he really did it." Silver, however, regards Crossley's Bar as a tiny part of his involvement at Dean Clough.

"I started letting space to quite a lot of people. By the time I left in August 1984 rental income was quite high. I was working from 8am to 6pm in the office and from 6pm to midnight in the bar. Ernest felt morally obliged to turn up in the bar because I was there and we were 50-50 partners, but I don't think he was interested in it.

"He had just sold out at Mountleigh and was a millionaire. I was just very young and affluent, not a millionaire. My energy was burning in a way that people find very exhausting. My motivation was to turn a rabbit-warren of a building into a dynamic, thrusting enterprise. I set about selling retail space, working closely with Ernest's son Jeremy, who had no shares in the business at that time.

"Apart from leasing space, my main objective was regeneration, putting life back into the mill. I see it as my testing ground, not a blueprint, a learning ground where I cut my teeth on Millstone Grit.

"I did a full-page advertisement in the Halifax Courier which said: 'Back to work at Dean Clough', which listed all the firms there. I used Saatchi and Saatchi through a mate of mine in Manchester. The main purpose was to say, 'This is not a white elephant'. I think Ernest probably forgets this because his vision of the way it went from there was to become so personal and evangelical. My vision was totally different.

"The reality was I was tiring Ernest out with my enthusiasm, arrogance and energy. I didn't want to do that because I liked him. I was also getting pretty tired myself."

When they were in partnership life was exciting but taut with unresolved tensions. Opposites may attract in love, but in business they don't stay together long. Now that Sir Ernest and Jonathan are not in business together their respect for each other flows freely, unobstructed by proximity.

I lunched in Crossley's Bar with Sir Ernest in the summer of 1988. When I returned to Dean Clough one rainy September afternoon eight years later, it had gone.

Gaunt, grey and green, with a spectacular panorama of hills, Halifax reminds me of

El Greco's painting of Toledo. Halifax relies on the flattery of sunshine to lend it charm, or the majesty of thunder to give it drama.

The exterior of Dean Clough, whether in rain or sunshine, is not charming at all. But for the Englishness of the design, and the gigantic DEAN CLOUGH sign on the roof of the main block, the sprawling complex could easily be mistaken for an engineering works in what used to be the German Democratic Republic. In terms of physical beauty and splendour of setting, Salts Mill wins hands down, as I think Sir Ernest would concede.

He would also be quick to point out, however, that he has spent a great deal of money on Dean Clough's interior which, I must say, is splendid.

The location of the former partners renews the historical link between Dean Clough and Salts Mill. Sir Titus's son, Titus Junior, married Katherine Crossley, daughter of John Crossley and niece of the Halifax MP Sir Francis Crossley. The Salts and the Crossleys were close friends. Titus Junior also organised experiments with the electric telephone, linking his home at Milner Field with Salts Mill and Crossley Mills (Dean Clough). Bradford historian Jack Reynolds, the source of this information, does not relate whether the ensuing series of trials were successful.

Internally, Dean Clough has changed beyond recognition since 1983. At the time of writing it is the base for 200 companies, and has six exhibition galleries and two theatre companies. Barrie Rutter's extraordinary Northern Broadsides theatre company, acclaimed throughout the country for its productions of classical drama, was the first professional company to be invited to stage a play at London's Globe Theatre. More than 20 artists-in-residence operate in Dean Clough which has a permanent collection of some 600 exhibits.

Sir Ernest's work in promoting business, the arts and manufacturing was recognised in December 1994 when Prince Philip presented him with the Royal Society of Art's Albert Medal. Previous recipients include the late Lord Olivier, and Yehudi Menuhin.

At the age of 65 instead of collecting his bus pass he recorded and released on CD four of the most difficult piano pieces written this century - the three Bartok Piano Concertos and Lutoslawski's Piano Concerto. Naxos, the world's third-largest producer of classical CDs, then signed him up to record Sir Arthur Bliss's Piano Concerto. Sir Ernest, born poor in Bolton, plays Bartok with the passion of an emigre Slav. His ambition is to record Chopin's complete piano works.

Looking back, Sir Ernest said Jonathan Silver could not be classified as a businessman because he did not think logically.

"Today's problems are not tomorrow's. He has an emotional reaction to things and that's difficult to relate to sometimes. I have seen him going through an emotional scene with some people about something that's so trivial as to be unbelievable. It's part of his personality, which has incredible strengths.

"He has tremendous visual understanding; he can get to the heart of things and see in a flash what people are doing; he has a sound instinct as to what's going to be popular.

"I would say he is a little boy that's never grown up.

"He's got a Jeykll and Hyde personality. On the one hand he can be incredibly generous; but on the other he can think in a very small-minded way."   Ernest Hall was undoubtedly the younger man's mentor, a father figure in some respects (Silver has never gone into business with his own father).

The difference in their personalities is reflected by the interiors of Dean Clough and Salts Mill. You could eat your dinner off the floor or carry out an operation in the pristine splendour of Dean Clough's main art gallery. The 1853 Gallery, by contrast, is crowded with objects. It is, as Silver says, an Aladdin's cave; it perfectly reflects the multi-faceted, discursive mind of its creator.

When Hall and Silver talk about one another do they contradict each other, or simply offer different perspectives? A rabbi once said that the opposite of one profound truth is not a lie but another profound truth.

"From my time with Ernest Hall I took every opportunity to learn from his brilliant understanding of business - disproving completely the theory that I don't listen to people. As a teacher he's got one thing in common with Hockney - he's great.

"Underneath his public veneer (which I don't have), he's very intense, single-minded, ruthless, domineering. He thinks very rationally: I don't think in that way. I can allow myself to become dominated by emotion: that's why I am not good at teamwork: that's probably why I am not very good at delegating as Ernest Hall is. But I like to think my energy makes up for it, and that I might become a bit more lateral as I get older; but I doubt if I will."   Hall and Silver's different ways of doing things led to the partnership splitting up. One of Alan South's favourite anecdotes perfectly illustrates the differences of personal style between the two friends.

"I have never forgotten a meeting we had with somebody wanting quite a lot of space. We were sitting in what used to be the boardroom, and Jonathan was there in his jeans, feet up on the table. The 'phone rang. Ernest and Jonathan both rushed to pick it up, but Jonathan grabbed it. All we could hear him saying was, 'Yuh, yuh, yuh. Right, I'm on my way!' He put on his shoes as he was going to the door, turned round and said: 'Sorry, got to go, the cat's ill!' The pained look on Ernest's face stays with me to this day."

Silver says it was inevitable that Ernest Hall would offer to buy his fifty per cent of Dean Clough since tension was mounting, and because his friendship with Hall was more valuable than partnership in business. Silver decided to sell his shares to Hall even though he says he was advised against doing so. The sum was substantial, enough for the restless Silver to consider a radical change.

"I just came home one day and said: 'We're going round the world!' Maggie thought it was great. We took Zoë and Davina out of school, we didn't know if we would be coming back. We sold absolutely everything - including the knives and forks. I was not far off being a millionaire."

The Silver family travelled and sojourned in the South of France, Southern Spain (where Jonathan's parents were then living), Kenya, South Africa, Sri Lanka, Japan, Australia, New Zealand, West Vancouver, California and Texas. They drove from California through Texas, clocking up five thousand miles.

Nearly three years out of Britain's school system affected Zoë so badly that in 1994 she passed all her GCE A Levels with top grades and went to Cambridge University. Ernest Hall's abiding belief that real education only takes place when personal qualities such as confidence and courage are allowed to grow and develop never had a better example. We can only really know what we love. Love, whether excitingly impassioned or soberly analytic, is the true conductor of wisdom and experience.

Travelling so extensively allowed Silver to give back to his family, whom he cherishes, some of the time he had poured into his business affairs.

11. PICTURES AT AN EXHIBITION

Thousands of people who visit Salts Mill accept as a matter of fact the enterprise's artistic and commercial success, as though that was guaranteed in the bill of sale.

The 37-year-old Silver started with nothing of the sort. He had an opportunity, nothing more; but much had to be done, and much money had to be spent, to turn opportunity to an advantage. Silver could have fallen flat on his face, and I dare say some people were hoping he would do so.

In my experience the fear of success is more prevalent than the fear of failure, which tends to unite the faint hearted in a like-minded community.

Just as Titus Salt had gambled on alpaca and had the guts to back his own judgement, Silver gambled on his ability to attract the public to a charming but down-at-heel Bradford suburb to visit an art gallery at the bottom of a hill. He opened in horrible November; admission was free of charge, as it still is. The public were drawn to it, as they still are in ever-increasing numbers.

Silver was not afraid of success, he relished it. The modern phenomenon of Salts Mill must be attributed to Silver's gift for making things happen. That's why he bought the mill in the first place.

"I made it clear at an early stage that the Gallery would be a place to meet, a focal point. David Hockney knew the mill very well as a kid. I got in touch with him again and asked if he would be kind enough to lend some pictures. I started buying his work very quickly at that point.

"We sponsored Opera North's production of West Side Story by a young director, Graham Vick, one of the most important opera directors now working. We must have given them a few thousand pounds because we gave them the oil to heat the weaving shed where Pace now have a factory. It made News at Ten and once again, Salts Mill was seen as a new place to go.

"People outside the area started remarking on this when they came to visit the Gallery. The day after I bought the mill I was offered £1million profit to sell it. It didn't even enter my mind to take it. The person at the other end of the phone was flabbergasted." Years later Silver was offered a lot more than £1 million profit to sell. He considered the offer, but not for long. He was enjoying himself too much, and also he felt a sense of responsibility to what he had started, and to what Titus Salt had created all those years ago.

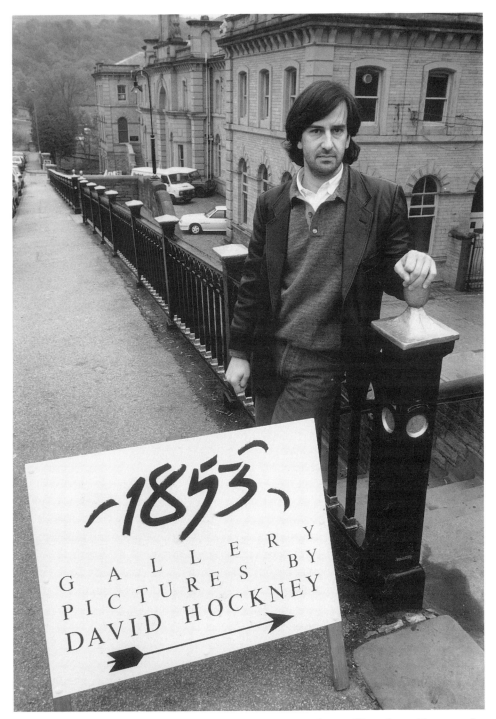

An art gallery opens in an empty factory in a run-down Victorian village at the bottom of a hill, three miles outside Bradford, and in horrible November. The beginning in 1987.

Photo: Telegraph & Argus

Paul Hockney, who has managed David's business affairs over the years, says Salts Mill now contains the biggest single collection of Hockney images in the world: original paintings, drawings, lithographs, photo-montages, photographs, prints and posters. Some were retrieved from the warehouse in Slough where Hockney's work is stored. Some belong to Bradford Council's arts and museums department. About 104 belong to the Hockney family, while Silver says he owns about 100 others.

The collection is constantly expanding as new works become available. In 1994, Silver purchased one of David Hockney's Very New Paintings, and Hockney's two series of 12 coloured lithographs. I happened to be at the mill on both occasions when the painting and six of the lithographs were delivered.

The painting came with five crates containing 71 crayoned drawings of Hockney's friends, family and dachshunds - which were to have their world premiere at Salts in July. That warm and sunny afternoon I became the first journalist perhaps in the entire world to have a good look at them. They were carried in two at a time and placed along the length of the gallery next door to the Diner. Among the portraits were six of Hockney's mother Laura. Silver put on the video of the pictures which Hockney had shot (he also chose the Palm Court orchestra soundtrack). The music, which recalled the age of Franz Lehar, was especially touching as I gazed down at the pictures of the woman with the lined and weathered face, almost as old as the century, and the almost supplicatory arthritic hands.

I counted no fewer than 23 drawings of the dogs, Stanley and Boodge. Not being a dog-lover or even a dog-fancier myself, I was taken aback by sheer canine quantity. Hockney had evidently devoted a great deal of time and attention to capturing the cute poses of his pets. Animals were coming back into fashion in art. Damien Hirst had put a dead shark in a glass case of formaldehyde, calling it The Impossibility of the Idea of Death in the Mind of Someone Living. He followed that up with half a cow and a calf, anticipating ironically the slaughter of British cattle to come in the mad cow furore. By contrast, Hockney's drawings of Stanley and Boodge, reminiscent of Ernest Shepard's Winnie the Pooh illustrations, were witty and affectionate.

The exhibition, accompanied by a catalogue which Silver had persuaded Hockney to do as well, ran for six months and then transferred to America. Astonishingly, Salts Mill is sometimes the only place in Europe where one can see a new Hockney exhibition.

The lithographs arrived one Saturday morning in December. Silver placed them in the 1853 Gallery. As though arranging them on the walls of his mind, he restlessly walked up to them and then stepped back ."They are so beautiful," he said when I asked him to explain the attraction.

"He really wasn't doing it as a commercial venture at first," says Paul Hockney. "I think he was trying to get Salts Mill on the map, and now it's on the map because of the Hockney Gallery. He'll say it's not a commercial venture now; he just says he likes it and likes the Press."

Sir Ernest Hall, whom Silver consulted before buying Salts, thinks Silver may have

Relaxing in his 1853 Gallery in May 1992, surrounded by the biggest collection of David
Hockney images in the world. *Photo: Telegraph & Argus*

started out with the intention of creating his own version of Dean Clough.

"The only difference was in the style in which he did it. There was also a small
business park in part of the mill. But bit by bit he got rid of it which, I think, was a
master stroke because I think he achieved more success. The big difference was the
locale.

"Being on the tourist trail gave Salts a much greater potential. He got in an architect
to look at the possibility of a major retail development, but the relationship came to a
stormy end. I think a major capital spend with retail would have been a hazardous
commitment.

"The Hockney Gallery was the first thing he really did. He always was a Hockney
devotee ever since I first knew him. I think his relationship with David Hockney and
Tony Harrison is what makes Salts work for him.

"If he were an artist he would be getting that nourishment directly. That ability to
respond to creative artists means a tremendous amount to him."

A tremendous range of Hockney merchandise is on sale at Salts. T-shirts, baseball caps, calendars, postcards, posters, a host of books, find a ready market among the stream of visitors from all over the world. On three different days I have seen parties of Japanese, Americans and South Africans, with a very satisfied-looking Silver standing behind the arrangement of desks that serve as the 1853 Gallery's counter.

Books and postcards of other artists' work abound too; but Hockney's predominates.

Hockney himself, who views the world more compassionately as he gets older, is mildly amused by Silver's eye for a marketable opportunity. He regards the various products bearing his name or motif as necessary advertising. For 20-odd years Hockney has lived in the USA, the land of advertising. He's used to it. He also receives royalties from some of the merchandise and art works.

The main thing is that his work is magnificently displayed all round the Gallery, hanging from pipes, jostling with lavish plants, antiques, wonderful vases, and the odd bit of junk which has caught Silver's eye; and to set everything off there is a constant soundtrack of classical music, usually Wagner. With the exception of the interior of Bradford's ancient Cathedral and York Minster, the 1853 Gallery is the most peaceful and civilised place I know. It is spiritually uplifting - a peculiar achievement for a self-proclaimed atheist.

Since 1988, an ever-expanding range of books has been on sale in the Gallery. Most of them are laid out flat on an assortment of 40-odd surfaces, including spacious window recesses and a large butcher's block which took Silver's fancy in 1994. The advantage of this novel method of display is that the browser does not get a chronic Hunchback of Notre Dame crick in the neck from trying to read the spines. There are thousands of titles, covering fiction, the classics, travel, art, poetry, feminist and gay writing, plays, motion picture scripts, psychology, music, philosophy, history, biography, as well as a varied array of children's books. In addition, there are upwards of 30 racks or tables covered with fine art cards. Words, music, pictures, carpets, glass cases, cabinets, flowers, magnificent vases, and the odd bit of junk, tumble into each other. There is none of the usual compartmentalisation one finds in libraries and traditional galleries. The interior reminds me of a Chagall painting, where objects defy the rules of physics, obeying only the imagination.

Without Hockney's pictures, however, the Gallery would have remained just a good idea.

Silver is a passionate collector of the extraordinary 'Arabian Nights' vases made in Leeds between 1885 and 1904 by the Leeds Fireclay Co. Ltd. - better known as Burmantofts.

He fell in love with these large wonderfully-coloured objects as a student. Upwards of 100 pieces are now on view in the 1853 Gallery, and in the gallery upstairs, making Silver the largest single private collector possibly in the country. Their intricately-patterned oriental designs reflect Victorian England's obsession with the Indian Sub-Continent. The warm olive greens, citrons, dark blues, Persian blues and brilliant turquoise fired Silver's imagination.

An exhibition of Anglo-Persian Burmantofts in Saltaire's Victoria Hall in 1887

This Burmantofts Faience vase c 1885 just one of Silver's amazing collection on show in the 1853 Gallery. *Photo: Salts Estates*

included a vase more than four feet in height which, by lucky chance, Silver discovered and bought in London in November 1994. The story perfectly illustrates the way his mind works - making connections between disparate experiences and circumstances.

"When I was in my first year at Leeds University I bought some Burmantofts from an antiques shop called Woodruff Antiques, beneath the Roundhay Clock cinema, not having a clue that years later I would be paying £11,400 for a vase exhibited at Saltaire.

"I went to London to an auction at Christies with the intention of buying some William Morris tapestries. I bid up to £15,000 for the one I wanted. An agent for Andrew Lloyd Webber bought it for £165,000. I later found out he bought all the tapestries for about £1 million, because Webber is putting together the biggest collection of Victorian and Pre-Raphaelite art ever.

"I wandered up to Bond Street and found myself in the Fine Arts Society. As I walked in through the door the first thing I saw was this huge Burmantofts vase. I couldn't believe how big it was. They told me they had just paid £6,500 for it - and they told me that before I made them an offer. Initially they wanted £18,000, which I said was ridiculous. After negotiations, which lasted about two minutes, they accepted my offer of £11,400, but still made a profit of £4,900.

"This is an important lesson in business: you shouldn't be worried about people making a profit out of you.

"One hundred and seven years after the vase was exhibited at Victoria Hall it ends up back in Saltaire in the 1853 Gallery. I find that deeply interesting."

With the 1853 Gallery established, Silver's next idea to give the mill national significance was to persuade the Victoria & Albert Museum in London to locate part of its marvellous South Asian art collection there.

Sir Roy Strong, then director of the V&A, came to Saltaire and was so impressed he declared it was "the Chelsea of the North". Had Strong remained in charge Silver may well have got his way; but Sir Roy retired and Elizabeth Esteve-Coll took his place.

A group of V&A trustees including Clifford Chetwood and Lord Armstrong, Mrs Thatcher's former Cabinet Secretary whose phrase "economical with the truth" during the notorious Spycatcher trial is now part of the language, came to look round the mill in 1988. The building, still largely empty, evidently did not impress them.

Both Silver and Alan South got the impression that these panjandrums were less than keen for thousands of the V&A's priceless artefacts to go on show in a former factory. Silver, however, was so convinced that Salts was the ideal location that he set aside a large space and talked a Yorkshire public company into offering £1 million to sponsor the project. Silver himself was prepared to offer a peppercorn rent. He believed that this, together with Saltaire's beautiful scenery, the elegance of the building and the flourishing 1853 Gallery, would be sufficient to sway the sceptical trustees. Plans were being made elsewhere, however.

The political balance of power in Bradford's City Hall had altered since Sir Roy Strong's enthusiastic visit in July 1987. Bradford's Labour Group had lost overall control of the council in the May elections, but held on to the chairmanships of important committees by virtue of a one-year agreement with the minority Social and Liberal Democratic Party. In June, however, Labour lost a by-election in Odsal ward and, critically, on September 15th they lost another by-election in the same place. Power fell into the hands of the Conservative Group led by Councillor Eric Pickles.

The Tories were only able to sustain this position by politicising the office of Lord Mayor (who happened to be a Conservative that year), ordering him to use his second and casting vote to pass controversial legislation at policy-deciding meetings of the full council.

Within months of the Tories gaining control, a fantastic scheme was unveiled by a rival Bradford mill only a couple of miles away from Salts, a scheme which had the backing of both Bradford Council and the Department of Environment.

Lister and Co., which ran the 55-acre Lister's Mill, a largely disused textile mill with a gigantic chimney, announced plans to incorporate the V&A's South East Asian Collection in a walled leisure complex which was to include a hotel, shops, flats, and offices. The estimated cost was £67 million The announcement was made on

November 30th, 1988, at a Press conference.

Silver, who had heard on the grapevine that a rival bid was in the wind, decided to attend it.

"Alan South and myself went to the Press conference at Lister's which was called by Justin Kornberg, president of the company. We had wind of the fact that our offer was going to be spurned. Bearing in mind that it's not easy to spurn £1 million and free space, we went along.

"Before it started I was told that Justin Kornberg wanted to see me. Alan remained seated. Kornberg told me I could not stay. I said it was a public press conference, but he said he didn't want me there. I asked him why. All he did was to invite me to lunch in London - a meeting, by the way, which I have never had. I was then escorted out of Lister's, not aggressively but firmly, by a lady.

"The whole thing was extraordinary. It was clear how guilty Justin Kornberg felt. Salts had been screwed by Lister's. What was ironic was that they forgot Alan was in the meeting." Alan shrewdly kept his mouth shut and stayed in the meeting. Afterwards he reported in full to Silver. Paul Hockney, experienced in the political manoeuvres of City Hall, says the decision to persuade the V&A to go to Lister's was political. Alan South concurs with that view.

"Ronnie Farley (the Conservative's chairman of the Enterprise and Environment Committee), stood up at the Press conference and gave this spiel about the V&A and Lister's. From the Tories' point of view it was a brand new initiative to announce, inner-city regeneration: that was what was in it for then, I think. Jonathan wasn't upset; but he felt very very miffed about the way he had been treated." The Lister's scheme, portentously called Lister City, got enormous and supportive publicity.

On January 27th, 1989, the V&A announced its preference for Lister City, following the presentation of a feasibility study costing £37,000 paid for jointly by the V&A, Bradford Council and the Department of Environment. Yet more glowing publicity followed. The paper plan was taken for reality. The people of Bradford were told that by 1993 Lister City would be ready for opening.

David Trippier, Under Secretary of State at the Department of Environment, visited Lister's Mill on March 15th and formally opened the Lister City Project to the Public.

That July Bradford Council's Planning Sub-Committee gave the project its blessing, but nothing happened.

On March 18th, 1991, with Labour now back in power in City Hall, the Government offered a grant of £10 million towards the project. Lister and Co. had asked for £17 million.

The economic climate had changed since the heady days of November 1988 when the whole country was in the grip of a Treasury-fuelled boom; now the country was in the teeth of the worst recession since the 1930s, hardly a time for grandiose schemes.

In January 1992 Lord Armstrong, chairman of the V&A trustees, sent a letter to Justin Kornberg in which he said the proposed museum was unlikely to get the £21 million necessary to turn the paper plan into reality. Quite simply, the V&A which had chosen the Lister City scheme in preference to Salts Mill, couldn't afford to stump up its share of the cash. Kornberg chose to look on the bright side, declaring that the project was not dead. But Ronnie Farley, now leader of the Tory Group, had had a private meeting with the-then Environment Secretary Michael Heseltine at a Warwickshire hotel and knew that the writing was on the wall.

"It is very bad news for Bradford," he told the Press. "This decision by a cosy group of London-based grandees is typical of the blinkered Southern bias that still exists within the arts. Their decision shows a complete ignorance of life outside the capital."

Was Farley deflecting attention from the fact that the Council had backed a loser? Even with the offer of £10 million from the Department of Environment the Lister City project failed to materialise. Farley denies there was any "back-dealing" between the Council and Justin Kornberg to keep Jonathan Silver out.

"We would have been happy to have backed either scheme. The interest the V&A showed in Lister's in Manningham was because of the geographical location - its high Muslim population.

"It was the V&A which decided it wanted to be at Lister's. At the time people thought, rightly or wrongly, that the V&A were going to fund their own museum. I think Esteve-Coll said very quickly, 'You do know we cannot afford to fund this scheme?' One of the great problems was that in the mid-1980s, when the scheme was drawn up, the economy was booming; but in 1988 the economy dive-bombed and in 1989 the housing market fell apart, and with it a good section of the Lister project. At the end of the day it just looked like a museum."

The economy was actually still buoyant in 1988, the year that the Lister City scheme was announced. If the V&A did indeed make clear that it could not afford to contribute to the multi-million pound scheme, why on earth didn't somebody say something?

Silver, who has little respect for politicians, perhaps suffers for his unconventional mode of operation; less imaginative people mistake it for dreamy unreality. Dreaminess is not part of his make-up. Today Salts flourishes whereas Lister's is two-thirds empty, dilapidated, and a regular target for vandals.

There was talk of applying to the National Lottery for funds to revive the 70-acre Lister City project. Then in May 1995 a Liverpool development company announced that it had bought the South complex for £1.6 million, and hoped to spend £35 million converting it into homes, shops, and a museum.

The V&A plan was finally junked. That was followed by the collapse of the scheme which replaced it.

12. DAVID AND JONATHAN

Although the V&A's decision in January 1989 was a profound disappointment, Silver wasn't one to sit around and mope. Within 11 months he pulled off an astonishing coup which attracted publicity from Los Angeles to Sydney for Salts Mill and David Hockney.

Hockney, ever the experimenter, was playing about with fax machines. Artists are generally thought of as technological Luddites, hostile to soulless and soul-destroying machinery. Hockney was never that. Always ready to try his hand at something new, he was intrigued by the possibilities of fax machines which, he noted, were regarded as subversive in Communist countries.

Hockney had already caused a stir by transmitting four very large pictures by fax to Sao Paolo, Brazil. In September 1989, in response to questions faxed to him by Brazilian journalist Pepe Escobar, Hockney faxed back his answers which included the following:-

"I've noticed fountain pens are being advertised again (ten years ago you could only buy them in an art store). It is also spreading printing machines around - the first victims of this seems to be the totalitarian world (you cannot buy an office-copier in Eastern Europe because if you could you'd have a free press). This deeply appeals to my anarchistic heart." In Los Angeles, Silver saw copies of the pictures faxed to Brazil and asked Hockney to send a fax to Salts Mill. "I'll send one tomorrow, if you want," Hockney replied.

Sensing a golden opportunity, Silver persuaded the artist to hold his horses. What he wanted was a major media event; either by luck or judgement chose the right day for it.

Thursday November 10th, 1989 was historic in more ways than one. Two years and nine days after the Gallery had opened with a modest show of 53 Hockney pictures, several hundred invited guests arrived for one of the most exciting and unusual evenings of their lives.

Conversation was dominated by the news from East Germany. The Government of the German Democratic Republic had surprisingly given permission for its citizens to travel freely. The Berlin Wall was history. The decision had been made on the ninth, but the full impact of what it meant did not register in Britain until the following day. Early evening TV news programmes that wet and wild Thursday were dominated by pictures from East Berlin. Silver's guests were in a state of excitement and euphoria before they even entered the 1853 Gallery and saw the TV cameras, and the milling flux of national newspaper photographers.

In a specially prepared space were two plain paper fax laser printers, loaned by the Japanese company Ricoh, a huge acid-free rag board, and two stepladders painted in transverse stripes of red, white and blue - reminiscent of Hockney's stage props for Parade.

Thousands of miles away in sunny Los Angeles, Hockney got ready to transmit 144 segments of picture via satellite to the town from where, 102 years earlier, Titus Salt Junior had sent a telephone message to Halifax. Hockney's studio was an oasis of calm and tranquillity compared with the party atmosphere in the Gallery.

Just after 7pm the first fax came through. Two hours later Silver pressed the final segment in place and everyone cheered. The completed picture was the size of a bus and called Tennis - clearly recognisable by bits of netting, the grain of the court, and black and white balls. The event was covered by CBS, YTV, The Economist, the Sydney Morning Herald, The Observer, The Times, the now-defunct Sunday Correspondent, The Daily Telegraph, The Guardian, The Independent, The Yorkshire Post and the Telegraph & Argus. Silver the showman couldn't have been happier.

On a never-to-be-forgotten night when the world saw the fall of the Berlin Wall, he had proved that he could make things happen.

Hockney memorably described fax as the "telephone for the deaf". Profoundly deaf himself, he would have appreciated the historical coincidence of sending a fax to the mill built by a man born in 1803 - the year deaf Beethoven finished the Eroica Symphony.

'Tennis' was not the first piece he had done for Silver. Twenty-six years earlier, in the summer of 1963, Class 4G at Bradford Grammar School were putting together a magazine. As one of the three appointed editors Silver, then 13, came up with the audacious idea of asking former BGS pupil David Hockney to design the cover. He obtained Hockney's Bayswater telephone number, a feat in itself, and rang him. Then he wrote what Hockney later told me was a "strong, cheeky letter".

Eventually the 25-year-old golden boy of contemporary British art met Jonathan one Thursday afternoon in Sydney Silver's Bradford Wimpy Bar. Jonathan remembers Hockney turning up in a two-piece Madras suit, green shirt, pink tie, odd socks, outrageous shoes, and black-framed John Ogden glasses. After the meeting, which went well, Silver hurried home to Wilmer Drive to tell his mother what had taken place.

"He came home and was brimming over with joy and went into great detail about how David was dressed that day. I looked at him and said, 'God Jonathan, I hope he doesn't fancy you!'"

On July 16th Hockney, who was finishing his Rake's Progress etchings, sent Silver a short letter and the requested cover design - "a sort of variation of the school tie". Jonathan got his first bit of publicity and Bradford Grammar School got Hockney's design.

Their next meeting took place five years later in 1968.

David and Jonathan, making things happen in Salts Mill.   *Photo: Telegraph & Argus*

Hockney, just turned 30, had made a splash with his paintings of Californian swimming pools. He was in the middle of a series of finely executed pen and ink drawings, which included a memorable portrait of W.H. Auden, his wedding cake face already beginning to crumble, and Hockney's favourite model Celia Birtwell.

Silver, 18, recently back from a futile term at Enfield College of Technology, had decided to become an artist. He was furiously chucking paint at canvases in his upstairs studio at 17a Barry Street at night, and working in the Wimpy Bar during the day. Hearing that David was due to lecture at Bradford College of Art, he invited him to Barry Street.

"It was the first time I had seen him since I was 13. He did come to the studio and advised me about painting, as he still does. He took me out to a pub in Bradford that evening where there was a male drag show going on."

"I think David is a little bit frightened of him because if Jonathan wants anything doing he's like a terrier," says Hockney's brother, Paul. "But he says he's never met anyone like Jonathan. At one time he used to go through me to get David to do things. Now he goes direct.

"When he went over to Los Angeles at the time of the New Drawings (1994) he persuaded David to write the introduction to the catalogue and stood over him while he did it. David says to me, 'It's like being in school with the teacher standing over me, telling me what to do'."

Hockney clearly admires Silver's energy, recognising a kindred spirit. Silver has made his way in the world by doggedly being himself. Like Silver, Hockney has a low boredom threshold and needs a regular supply of fresh challenges. Whether you share Silver's estimation of Hockney as an artist, you have to concede that he is the most inventive and hard-working living artist in the world. But what does David say about Jonathan?

"He's a little bit mad is Jonathan, but you need someone a bit mad to do this (stage sensational happenings at Salts Mill). You need some energetic, slightly mad person.

"He does have an eye, he likes painting and drawing; it isn't as though he is a person who doesn't know the difference between things. He has a visual side, the visual arts are a stimulant to him. He uses it to get people here and so, in that sense, it has put the place on the map.

"Jonathan is forever pushing something in front of you, but you've got to do it immediately, and he knows you'll do it quick. He's always got pens in his pocket.

"He owned a lot of prints and if somebody owns a lot of prints they can hang them where they want. But as he developed it (Salts Mill) and put books in and postcards I thought, 'It's a lively place and gets an awful lot of people.' "

Hockney was speaking to me off-the-cuff on a rainy Saturday night in December 1994, the 17th. He was at Salts to take part in a charity evening, which subsequently raised more that £30,000 to buy hospital equipment for sick children. He had agreed to take part in a question and answer session with the audience of 200.

Tony Harrison and playwright Alan Bennett, who were also taking part, made up the triumvirate of Yorkshire-born artists. Bennett, often mistaken for Hockney, was to give a reading from his diaries, Alan Bennett: Writing Home, in the new Hockney Gallery - a Florentine-style room painted aquamarine and rust-red which Hockney had designed using a scale model. He and Hockney had not met for 16 years. You wouldn't have thought so, for after the show they sat laughing over dinner like Mole and Ratty in The Wind in the Willows, or two mischievous schoolboys who had just booby-trapped the physics teacher's Bunsen burner.

I had arrived at the mill an hour or more before Bennett was due to start. Hockney was in the Diner, two floors above the 1853 Gallery, giving an interview to Michael Church. I had come to arrange an interview for this book at a later date, but Silver, sensing that his friend was in a highly receptive mood, suddenly asked Hockney if he wanted to do the interview there and then. After a moment's reflection, David nodded his head. With that Silver ushered everyone out. "This is private!" he said, sweeping them away, enjoying the drama of it.

Supplied with bitter beer and red wine, Hockney was disposed to be loquacious. I contented myself with following his line of thought, interrupting periodically to make a point.

Three Hockneys together: David, brother Paul, and mother Laura.   *Photo: Jonathan Silver*

"If you were going on the moors as a child you would walk by this mill. People would take a bus to Saltaire, walk down here or go by the Glen road, or walk over Ilkley Moor. You're talking about the 1940s and 1950s when people didn't have cars. The mill was very active then. All I can remember was the noise from it: the engines, the belt-driven looms. So when Jonathan told me he had got this mill I said 'I know it'; I've known it since I was six years old.

"At first he put up pieces of my work he owned and borrowed pieces that my mother had kept. I didn't know she had, but mothers keep everything don't they? Then I suggested to Paul, OK he's done it, I will find him a few things. Actually he made Bradford seem much more lively. Suddenly the mill grew and grew and I saw what he was doing here. I knew it was a way of getting attention for the place."   I asked him if he had minded that. Did he think Silver was using his work for his own purposes, or was he displaying it for its own sake?

"I realised he was doing both. I think I told him about Minneapolis. I was there doing a theatre show in 1983 and in Minneapolis they have some big grain warehouses. They started transforming them instead of knocking them down, putting in shops, restaurants.

"No one knew what to do with Salts Mill, it seemed like a white elephant. By putting in something to see for people who would come by, it did draw attention - I knew that very well. But on the other hand I am a Bradfordian, two little Hockneys were born here in Bradford in 1993, my roots are here - unlike Tony Richardson, the film director, who came from Shipley. I used to say to him in Hollywood, 'Why don't you go back to Shipley?' and he would say, 'I have no reason to go, I have no family; I will go if you go', but he never did.

"I could see what Jonathan was going to do, that it would all take time and money, and somehow or other he had to put it on the map again and make something of it. He's now employing people again and in a different way. In the past when people were employed here their jobs were extremely dreary; people learned to lip read because of all the noise."

Alan Bennett once surprised me by saying how much he enjoyed being in America, especially New York. I had forgotten that he had played Broadway with the Beyond the Fringe satirical revue in the 1960s and assumed that God's own country would not be his cup of tea. But like Hockney he enjoys the vivacity if not the violence of America. I asked David how Jonathan got on with polluted Los Angeles.

"He comes for two days at most," he replied, and laughed.

"The last time we were putting on the show for my drawings (Friends and Best Friends). I had an idea of doing the catalogue from the video. Now he knows nothing about dogs. I have two. I am a person who doesn't go out much so they mean a lot to me, they sleep with me. So when I was drawing them I said to Jonathan, 'We could do this show of the dogs and call it Friends and Best Friends'.

"I suggested doing a poster of the dogs, and only when he put it up he discovered that other people are mad about dogs, and it was reviewed in Dog World, and that brought in a whole lot of dog owners who brought in their dachshunds. He discovered there was an enormous number of people with dogs who liked pictures. That was a whole area that was a bit new to him. Then he did a dog calendar. I said, 'Do it next year', but he wanted it for this year (1994). He wants everything this year."   Doesn't Jonathan's insistence on having things done so quickly sometimes get on his nerves?

"I might say to him, 'Oh it's not a good idea', and if I say that he knows I mean it. But on the other hand I respect his energy. What he's done in Bradford is wonderful. He puts on a play that he gets Tony (Harrison) to do that's terrific.

"Also, I'm sympathetic to his way of showing paintings and drawings that aren't for sale except as posters and postcards, so people aren't intimidated by what something is worth. They don't know, don't want to know. You can always take something away with you that's nice.

"I remember they had a marvellous Van Gogh exhibition at the Met in New York - Van Gogh at Arles. I had driven into New York and came back to Ken Tyler's, just outside New York, next morning.

"He said, 'It was terrific', but he said wasn't the end room terrible, where they were selling posters and scarves. I said, 'No, I bought one of the posters of Van Gogh's bedroom for 20 dollars. Van Gogh would love it, that for 20 dollars you could take a marvellous reproduction of one of his paintings home. I am surprised at you Ken, a printer, saying that'. He went back to the exhibition and said, 'Yes, I can see what you mean'. I pinned that poster up in my bedroom, saw it every morning when I woke up. I liked that. I had been to the exhibition and took away a very good reproduction of a painting.

"In a way that's what Jonathan has done here. He realises that there wouldn't be many people who could buy the drawings anyway, so in a sense he spreads it around. I am amazed that artists don't do them more - have posters. After all, most people know my work through books and I make sure the books keep coming out.

"I made the point that if we didn't have printing we wouldn't know about painting, and it's that aspect Jonathan also knows about, he knows about the philosophical side. On the other hand he has to make some money here, and it's one personality that's done it - not a committee sitting in the town hall.

"You simply have to advertise things because otherwise people don't know they're there. A mill in Bradford doesn't sound very inviting, but it's actually in a very beautiful location isn't it? By the canal, the river and the moors. A few friends from the States come here now, they come from London now. They are all knocked out, very surprised at the scale of the place.

"I must admit I am a person, kind of not outside the art world but sceptical of it; it doesn't reach out: that's why I say make posters. I have always thought that for years the art world is very small, yet the public appetite for pictures is actually very large.

"Some people think that if it's boring it's art. I have never taken that attitude. If it's boring to me it's not art. I admit I like some things people don't rush to. I don't say that everything is for masses and masses of people. In the end most art is forgotten. The only art that gets preserved is something somebody loves; love has to come into it. Rembrandt is always popular, Van Gogh is universally loved.

"The first big Van Gogh exhibition was in 1900 and the public flocked to it (critics didn't like it). That's why to me Van Gogh is one of the very greatest artists, because he speaks so directly to people. But I am aware that people won't give time to it, if it is a question of time. Still, in that sense I am a professional artist and am perfectly willing to give people time.

"I have always thought that people aren't as dumb as television executives think they are. I know the world is a bit mad out there, I have always thought that; but there's a lot of good will, a lot of people who know what's important in that sense. Most people know what's truly important; but that is the source of art, is it not, the source of curiosity?"

In a bumptious moment I once declared that Hockney was like Picasso: the older he got the more of a piss-taker he became.

Silver looked at me sharply and replied quietly: "I think you'll find David has more compassion and humanity than Picasso." The remark was meant to be corrective rather than admonitory. Hockney's observation that love must play a part in making art meaningful is as good a starting point as any.

Since the summer of 1985 I have interviewed the artist more than half-a-dozen

times. In every instance he was surrounded by acquaintances, art groupies, people eager to bathe in the reflected glory of his fame. He did his best to behave courteously to all, signing autographs and replying to questions about art and painting - the best questions to ask him. Though his reputation as an enfant terrible went before him he behaved like any other person in strange company.

In later years his shyness was more pronounced. Until he acquired a pair of sophisticated Swiss hearing aids in 1994, deafness in both ears had made crowded rooms intolerable. He avoided unnecessary company whenever he could. That affliction and the loss of many close friends through AIDS caused Hockney to withdraw deeper into himself. His second volume of autobiography, That's the Way I See It, candidly discusses the intense loneliness he sometimes feels; but his Yorkshire upbringing won't allow him to wallow in it. Hockney is as tough as old boots.

As a gifted artist who loves to be busy, he sees his job as alleviating the despair of others by creating beautiful pictures, revealing the world's beauty.

Perhaps he shares Dostoyevsky's conviction that the world will be saved by beauty. It certainly won't be saved by the superficial grotesqueries of the late Francis Bacon, an early influence on Hockney. Faced with the unlikely choice of taking to a desert island any of Bacon's paintings or, say, Olivier Messiaen's wondrous Quartet for the End of Time, I'd like to think that Hockney would choose the music.

During the 40 minutes or so we had at Salts Mill that December night in 1994, Hockney more than once referred to his Bradford roots and their importance. Since the summer of 1985, the first time I met him, he has put much time and effort into doing things for Bradford - little good though this done him with the public at large. J.B. Priestley said Bradford was a good place for discouragement.

Despite sarcastic letters to the Telegraph & Argus about his Bradford telephone directory cover in 1989 and the stamp he designed for the Royal Mail in 1992, which was launched at Salts, Hockney has rarely denied his home town.

In 1985 he spent several days at the National Museum of Photography, Film & Television, demonstrating his joiner photographs. People were allowed to watch him taking the pictures and arranging them to his satisfaction. Six years later, Hockney returned to the museum to launch his Electronic Snaps exhibition. Again, he gave a practical demonstration of how the pictures were made, this time using a hand-held video stills camera and laser colour photocopier. That weekend he gave a lecture on photography.

He has designed brochure covers for Bradford Council and in 1989 contributed a two-page drawing to a book to be auctioned for the Cancer Research Campaign, thereby greatly enhancing its value (he was only asked to sign it).

In 1986 he designed a two-page colour motif for the Telegraph & Argus in support of the city's valiant but ultimately futile image-building campaign, Bradford's Bouncing Back! He waived his fee. The picture, the subject of more sarcasm in the

Opposite: Silver is also a brilliant photographer, as this clever montage of David Hockney and the writer Alan Bennett (often mistaken for one another) in Salts Diner demonstrates.

This gigantic fax called Tennis was faxed from Los Angeles by David Hockney to Salts Mill the very night the Berlin Wall fell.   *Photo: D. Mansell*

newspaper's letters column, was entered for the Royal Academy's summer exhibition in 1987. Ten thousand copies of the double-page spread were put on sale at 18p a time and reputedly, sold out.

In 1993, Hockney's Very New Paintings (there were 30) came to Salts - the only place in England where they were exhibited. "People in the South will be very jealous and they'll have to come here to see the show - a sort of homage to Hockney, which is something Bradford needs," Silver told me at the time. The paintings, varying in size from three feet by two feet to 12 feet by ten, came out of the stage designs Hockney did for Richard Strauss's opera Die Frau Ohne Schatten - The Woman Without a Shadow.

Silver estimated that 90,000 people visited the exhibition. Hockney takes figures like that with a pinch of salt. What impressed him most, he told me, were letters sent to him by schoolchildren from Bradford and Manchester.

"A name, a reputation, means nothing to them. They are not going to say they find a painting interesting if it isn't, because children don't lie. Schools sent me pictures based on my paintings and I thought it was wonderful. I wrote back to a lot of the schools. I just encouraged them to enjoy themselves painting."

In April 1996, after a visit to his old school, Hockney invited four A Level art students and their art teacher, Robert Walker, to spend a couple of weeks in his Malibu beach house. He had been told that they did not have the money to pay for air fares and accommodation, and this prompted him to make his offer. When they got there he invited them up to his house in the Hollywood hills where Ann Upton fussed over them, cooking shepherd's pie. Hockney took them into his studio on Santa Monica Boulevard, showed them his latest work, and spent a lot of time talking about art.

"It was absolutely incredible. Two weeks in paradise," Robert Walker told me later. "David is a very kind man. He couldn't have done more than he did for us. The lads haven't stopped talking about it. The work is just pouring out of them." At Hockney's suggestion Silver put this work on display in the very gallery where he had premiered Hockney's Family and Friends drawings.

Hockney's fame has undoubtedly helped put modern Bradford on the map. As I was putting this book together, Bradford and Ilkley Community College's School of Art, Design and Textiles was planning to mark the artist's sixtieth birthday and the city's Centenary by launching the Hockney Drawing Competition. They hope a top cash prize, handsome enough to put the competition in the same league as the Whitbread and the Turner, will eventually attract entries from across Europe.

Hockney's belief that the public's appetite for pictures is greater than is generally supposed has been vindicated at Salts Mill. Jonathan Silver's first initiative after buying the mill was the creation of the 1853 Gallery. Normally developers put in the business and then, as an after thought, add a bit of art for decoration. The role of Hockney's art has been central to the regeneration of an entire community. Arguably, without the Gallery there would have been no business.

The unconventionality of the mill's interior, the way one thing is contrasted with another, either compels attention or pleasantly distracts. Overall it has attracted. As long as David and Jonathan are around it will continue to draw a multitude of people from all over the world.

Once again, Salts Mill is an international phenomenon.

FOOTNOTE

In June 1997, a week after Bradford ignored its world famous son and gave the Freedom of the City to Baroness Barbara Castle, David Hockney was made Companion of Honour in the Queen's Birthday Honours List.

13. REGENERATION

On that cold January Friday in 1877, the Bradford through which Sir Titus Salt's funeral cortege rumbled resembled a necropolis. The hundreds of factory chimneys puncturing the harsh blue of the Northern sky were inactive only for that morning. Bradford was still an industrial powerhouse.

In the 1930s J.B. Priestley said prophetically that Bradford, a city with a past, had to have a future too. In the late 1950s the shape of that future was imposed by Stanley Wardley's road system which cut central Bradford into quarters. Glass and concrete boxes, "the improvements" as David Hockney calls them, were put up and many fine old buildings pulled down to accommodate them.

Bradford, with a natural panorama reminiscent of Prague, in places could be mistaken for the drabbest parts of post-war East Berlin.

The men responsible for this utilitarian brave new world, were so intent on creating a modern Bradford in their own image that they ruthlessly destroyed the city that had been created by others unafraid to think big and build grandly. As modern Bradford seedily slumped into depression - its textile and engineering industries reeling from foreign competition, decisions by distant multi-national parent companies, and then two recessions - old-fashioned Saltaire, its heritage intact, thrived and prospered. Modern industry was established in a large Victorian mill which nobody had wanted. Now it flourishes, flanked by those twin symbols of the first Industrial Revolution - the canal and the railway.

Silver's independence, unfettered by red tape, unhindered by endless committees or board meetings, has undoubtedly helped him to bring about the regeneration of Salts in less than eight years.

Can corporate bodies like councils or government agencies follow in the footsteps of Silver or Sir Ernest Hall? If the regeneration of post-industrial cities is possible can it safely be left in the hands of property developers? Few of them could be likened to the entrepreneurial artist as envisioned by Sir Ernest Hall.

"When old English industries decline and fall, the towns that bore them turn first to the three Ds - drink, dole and depression - and then to heritage trails, shopping malls and garden festivals ... Northern towns however, cannot survive solely on service industries.

"Those who find jobs stacking shelves of superfluous superstores will never share the dignity (nor the bruises) of predecessors who built peerless ships, legendary

The once derelict mill now thrives. On the right of the canal the refurbished New Mill restored by private enterprise. The Filtronic Comtek electronics factory, bottom right, built on surplus Salts Mill land. Up to 2,000 people now work in the three buildings.

Photo: Wood Visual Communications

locomotives and great civic buildings. But what hope is there today beyond fast food, edge-of-town shopping and escalating leisure?" Art, paintings, even sculpture, says Jonathan Glancey, answering his own question in a long and well-written piece for The Independent newspaper on July 27th, 1994. Glancey, the paper's architecture editor, left London to look at three regeneration projects in depressed areas of the North-East: the Baltic Flour Mills museum, Gateshead; the proposed National Glass Centre, Sunderland; and the £200 million redevelopment of Hartlepool Docks, which includes a branch of the Imperial War Museum designed by Sir Norman Foster. Unfortunately for Hartlepool the museum project fell through in 1996.

"Art and culture, as many European cities know, can be a commercial magnet. A sophisticated provision of museums and galleries, alongside a reliable civic infrastructure (from good state schools to integrated public transport systems), appears to boost urban economies," Glancey wrote.

The first lesson to be learned is that regeneration cannot be sustained by garden festivals and art shows alone - though it may be started by them. Glasgow, probably the most famous example of the corporate pursuit of culture, found this out the hard way.

Once renowned for its slums, drunks and razor-gangs, Glasgow carried its bad image with a swagger because the mills, factories and shipyards were busy. There was plenty of work, and plenty of other things going on to distract the attention. But the first recession in the early 1980s closed the shipyards, emptied the factories and brought the mills to a grinding halt.

The authorities refused to accept that their city had had its day. The drive to attract new business by changing the public's perception of Glasgow's image as a nasty place North of the Border was a valid and valiant response. Most Glaswegians seemed to accept the Glasgow's Miles Better campaign, and that made all the difference. In 1988 the city hosted the National Garden Festival. Two years later it basked in the glory of European City of Culture. Investment poured in; Glasgow became fashionable.

Unfortunately, the second recession in the late 1980s and early 1990s undid much of the campaign's good work.

"Glasgow in the Nineties faces an economic and social crisis. The marketing experiments of the past few years have failed to revive the local economy," wrote John Arlidge in the Independent on Sunday on October 2nd, 1994. Putting on plays in former shipyards was no substitute for investment in housing, fighting escalating drug addiction, and all the other problems of the post-industrial city.

One of Arlidge's interviewees said investment had to be made in the people first; genuine culture would follow in due course.

Marketing is obviously no good on its own; you have to have something worth marketing to begin with. I doubt that it does any good at all - except to those employed to do it. The benefits to the public have never been clear to me. Similarly, image-building campaigns will fail without a coherent long-term strategy for planning and investment. Well-intentioned sloganeering campaigns begin with inflated enthusiasm, lots of meetings, reports and publicity. Accentuating the positive is the order of the day. And so every far-fetched, ambitious and perhaps inappropriate scheme is given uncritical support. Anyone who dares to question whether the king's new clothes actually exist is accused of being negative. Every action prompts a reaction and at least one unforeseen consequence. The concerted attempt to always look on the bright side beguiles its proponents to assume that everyone is working from the same agenda. Unscrupulous developers, with an eye on land values, have an entirely different set of principles. Cities desperate to attract business are wide open to such people. How many times have well-meaning public officials and politicians been misled by glittering presentations? The more implausible the scheme the grander will be the presentation, the bolder the promises of future wealth and jobs. Regeneration, to be meaningful, requires input from experienced practitioners. Left to enthusiastic amateurs, it will either collapse like a line of dominoes or result in a series of rent-free or low-rent developments with the commercial advantage all on one side. Come the next wind of change, the developer will up and leave and the city will be back to square one.

Jonathan Silver does little advertising in the accepted sense. His modus operandi is to stage unique events of high quality which attract publicity, which in turn attracts business.

Gateshead, Hartlepool and Sunderland took the route in the early 1990s pioneered by Silver in 1987, and by Silver and Ernest Hall four years earlier.

Silver started off at Salts with 53 Hockney paintings, but knew that Man does not live by Art alone. In the past six or seven years he has combined commerce and culture in a setting which manages to be both sufficiently bohemian and stylishly upmarket to attract the monied middle-classes. The success of this strategy was acknowledged in 1994 when Salts Mill won the Arts Council's £5,000 Centres for Arts award. The point is usually missed that admission to the various galleries now open at Salts is free. As more and more public galleries and museums make a mandatory charge, or request a donation, Salts Mill remains one of the few places upholding that tradition. Silver, who is passionate about this, maintains a free admission policy without grant aid of any kind. He is able to maintain this policy because of the success of the commercial enterprises inside the mill. Silver's regeneration stands or falls by the successful interplay of commerce and culture.

He can afford to spend thousands buying original Hockneys, Lowrys, commissioning paintings by other artists such as Simon Palmer, as well as buying Burmantofts pottery for the mill. The growing rental income from letting space to successful companies allows him to pursue his vision. But it all began with a tremendous act of faith. In the words of Sir Ernest Hall's Arts Council lecture: "Prosperity only returns when pessimism is replaced by optimism and people become heroic not helpless."

Pace Micro Technology plc, Britain's pioneering company in digital technology for satellite receiving equipment, is the most successful. It was created in a Bradford back-bedroom in the early 1980s, and boomed throughout the rest of the decade. Pace became a public company in the summer of 1996.

The 1980s were the years of uninterrupted political power for Margaret Thatcher, who spoke fondly of traditional Victorian values but whose policies smashed much that was traditional. That's why untraditional enterprises, such as Pace, flourished. Her 11 years of power brought in a host of things never seen before in the UK. Videos, satellite TV, cordless telephones, fax machines, were just a few of the technological novelties which gushed from the cornucopia of Thatcherism, along with the test-tube babies, solvent abuse, City Technology Colleges, Herpes, Trident and cash points.

Thatcherism had its own nomenclature: yuppies, loadsamoney, dependency culture, privatisation, the spirit of free enterprise. In the South, would-be tycoons played the stock market and the property market and overnight made bank-busting fortunes. In the North, men like David Hood, Barry Rubery and Robert Fleming invested their time, energy and money in new technology.

Fleming, who served 11 years as a medic in the RAF, including a five-month tour in the Falklands in 1982, chanced to see a magazine advertisement for computer parts by Hood, who was running a TV repair shop by day and Pace Software Supplies at other times from his house in Bradford's Lidget Green. Fleming drove North to meet him.

Later he joined forces with Hood and his business partner Rubery. In 1985 Fleming, then 28, left the RAF and Pace moved into premises 6,500 square feet in size.

Pace now occupies more than 250,000 square feet in Salts Mill and the three men can measure their personal wealth in Ferraris. Hood alone made a £100m from the sale of some of his shares. Rubery left the company in February 1997. But why did Pace's directors, conscious of the company's modern image, choose a 19th Century textile mill for their base?

In a Bradford Bengali restaurant one rainy September night, Fleming, Pace's operations director, answered that question. On the lookout for warehousing space, he had already been to Lister's Mill but wasn't satisfied with the terms.

"We wouldn't be able to come and go as we wanted," he said. "There was some land off Cemetery Road, a site for a building; but it was only 35,000 square feet.

"I went down to Salts Mill in 1990 and Jonathan Silver took me around. I went back again and this time he gave me his big bunch of keys and said 'Look around'. I thought it was extraordinary from the very first meeting with him. I had heard about this guy with the gallery and there he was, full of enthusiasm for the building, probably a bit more manic in those days than he is now.

"Alan South came with us the second time and he seemed to know a lot about the building. I wouldn't say Jonathan was pushy or anything; we weren't the company that we are now; we had only just started a satellite product then. There was no edge to him, he was very easy going. As far as the commercial thing went it was, 'We'll come to a suitable arrangement', and he was flexible. He's recognised that we want this bit of space now and might want something else later."

Silver's income from Pace alone has grown to more than £500,000 a year and continues to rise as Pace expands. There are 15 other enterprises, employing upwards of 1,500 people, which also add to his bank balance, either through rent or sales. The mill's commercial success is reinvested into the fabric and contents of the buildings.

For 25 months until March 1995, Silver had a clothes store adjacent to the Diner. I well remember the winter's afternoon he showed me the huge empty space and told me of his intention to invest many thousands of pounds in decorating, equipping and stocking a men's wear store. Mills in Leeds and Bradford supplied the cloth for the suits, trousers, jackets and shirts which he intended to sell below the price in the High Street. Good quality clothes, he said, had become too expensive. He added:-

"The reason clothes became expensive was because High Street rents in the boom period of the 1980s became ridiculously expensive. The shops that are left have to work up to a 280 per cent mark-up because rentals are huge, then there are staff wages and other overheads. So if you own a building like this one, with no rent to

pay and you know something about clothes, it doesn't take a lot of imagination to work out that my overheads are going to be lower, so we can sell a suit for £100."

Clothing racks, cupboards, light shades, tables and other non-functionary objects were made from materials recycled from the old Salts Mill, including the large hook from the original mill crane, and a steel chimney cut up to make table legs. The integration of the old and the new delighted Silver. The store, however, proved only periodically profitable. In 1995 he leased the space to the fabric and furniture firm Skopos Design.

On the floor above Skopos shops selling quality designer clothes, including the Pollyana range by the top British Designer Rita Britton, and hand-made jewellery were established in 1996. The textile connection remains, the only difference being Silver neither designs the clothes nor sells them.

But Pace, its blue circular arrow logo familiar all over the world, has gone from strength to strength. In 1985 the company employed 30 people. Nine years later that had mushroomed to 900. In 1994 the annual turnover was £80m. In 1995 it was £100m. The following year it nearly doubled to £196m. Turnover for 1997 was expected to double again.

It is an international company with sales and distribution offices in Sweden, Dubai, South Africa, Germany, the United States, France, Denmark, Norway and Hong Kong. There are three sub-contracting manufacturing plants in Barnsley, Stoke and Poole in Dorset, and one each in Poland and Thailand. Additional factories are being sought in Thailand, Mexico, Brazil and Indonesia.

Pace made it's mark by making modems and then by mass-manufacturing and selling analogue satellite receivers, decoders and cable TV decoders to 64 countries, and ploughing back profits into the company, particularly in research and development. Ninety staff are involved in R&D. At the time of writing Pace's own branded items comprise about half of the company's sales.

The company also invested £5 million in converting a former weaving shed into a bright, airy factory bigger than a football pitch, with Matisse and Hockney prints all around the walls and fifteen-foot trees in large tubs.

Long-term investment in R&D and manufacture has paid off. Pace, which started life in David Hood's back bedroom, claims to be the only company in the world mass-producing digital decoders for cable and satellite TV - outstripping the mighty multi-nationals of both Japan and the United States. The company is now in pole position to win lucrative business from the multi-billion pound digital terrestrial TV decoder market in the UK.

Regeneration, if it is to be more than a flash in the pan, requires a coherent strategy involving both education and training. Automation, which is supposed to lead to the wholesale shedding of labour, actually needs a steady supply of skilled workers.

In October 1995 I dropped in to see Robert Fleming. During the course of our conversation he revealed, with some irritation, that he was having a terrible problem recruiting people locally. So much so that he was bussing in sixty workers every day from Castleford - about 25 miles from Bradford. He wasn't after scientists with PhD's, just people with the requisite literacy, numeracy and manual dexterity.

"I think the whole thing is indicative of the problem we have in this country, this shortage-of-skills gap. If Britain wants to do manufacturing it has got to equip people to do that. Manufacturing means investment; but accountants are running most of industry these days and they say you don't have to invest in capital equipment," he told me.

"A lot of people in Bradford who can read and write don't want to work in a factory. But factories are where manufacturing is done. We cannot have a manufacturing industry without people getting their hands dirty. If there's no manufacturing it's not surprising that colleges aren't training people. I have spent money training people; but if the local community had invested along the lines of discussions I had with Bradford and Ilkley Community College two years ago I wouldn't have to go to Castleford for workers."

Fleming said the college had had difficulty finding enough people to fill the right courses. At the same time Bradford's Training and Enterprise Council had declined to manage the paperwork of Pace workers undertaking National Vocation Qualification certificates, even though he had offered to pay the wages of a TEC worker to do this for him. The TEC, he said, claimed that the procedure was contrary to their operating rules and instead offered him £1,000 for every worker Pace got through the NVQ.

"I told the TEC, which is a Government quango, I didn't want the money, which is taxpayers' money anyway. So now we're having to work with a college in Lancashire which will do the paperwork that Bradford TEC won't do," Fleming said.

Public reaction in Bradford was not favourable to Pace. People who had once worked in engineering were particularly offended by the implication that they were unskilled. And then the company was known to be antipathetic to trades unions. I discovered, however, that Fleming was not alone. He had identified a problem common to others. A number of people involved in hi-tech electronics manufacturing, engineering, teaching and business development told me that not enough was being done in Bradford to take advantage of the growth of hi-tech manufacturing which, since 1990, had created about 2,000 jobs in the city.

Dr Tony Martinez, founder of MicroVitec and now boss of Chase Advance Technologies in Bradford, said that if regeneration was to be based on wealth creation then Bradford in particular and Britain as a whole had to be aligned in the direction of growth, which meant electronics. Across the world electronics was growing at the rate of 35 per cent a year.

"Most universities and technical colleges cannot afford to have the facilities where students can learn about hi-tech manufacturing. Most graduate engineers don't have practical experience of manufacturing. Bradford does have a skilled workforce, but there's just not enough. Nowadays if you are going to employ an engineer you have to surround him with £100,000-worth of hi-tech kit. You need skilled and experienced workers to service, program and maintain hi-tech machines," he said.

"If Bradford is going to compete with other parts of Britain, it has got to help industries like Pace. Bodies which give out public money to train the unemployed have a rule book, but if that rule book doesn't support the needs of industry it should be put in the dustbin." Bradford, once the wool capital of the world, once again has to think in global terms. It is up against the likes of Japan which has a policy of long-term investment in Technopoli - large centres which bridge the gap between school education and training for work in the hi-tech industries of the 21st Century.

"I think that what is happening is that companies are growing faster than productivity growth, which means they need more people with the right skills. There's a limit to the amount of in-house training that companies can do," I was told by David Lloyd, Professor of Industrial Technology at Bradford University. "We need strategies to attract manufacturing industry. Education in these hi-tech areas should produce a new level of informed understanding of people in Bradford and provide a pool of people to work in these industries."

One Bradford firm, Filtronic Components, has resorted to sponsoring maths and science courses in five upper schools, hoping to encourage bright sixth-formers to take maths and science at GCE A Level. Part of this incentive, which is costing up to £80,000 over three years, includes ten weeks' paid work during the summer holidays at the company. Many other companies, including Pace, are either donating hi-tech equipment to schools or are engaged in joint venture projects combing the theoretical and the practical. In November 1996 the Daily Mail published an article about maths skills. Thirteen-year-olds in England and Scotland, it said, came out bottom in a group of 11 industrialised countries. Youngsters in Singapore were top of the league with an average of correct answers of 79 per cent, way above the international average of 55. England scored 53 and Scotland 52.

I find it strange that a city with Bradford's manufacturing history should boast of its IMAX cinema screen, but at the time of writing has yet to establish a Technopolis. Nineteenth Century textile manufacturers had more foresight. When their designs fell behind those of foreign competitors schools of art and design were created. Bradford does not need yet more graduates with humanities degrees to talk about its problems. It needs engineers, innovators, inventors.

The fragmentation of education has not helped. Schools and institutions of higher education which have to compete for funding according to the number of students they attract cannot afford to be selective about the courses they offer. If those courses tend towards the liberal arts and humanities then industry is bound to suffer. An all-round education should include both arts and sciences. For too long in this country these disciplines have been regarded as alternatives. Nowhere is this more marked than in poetry. In Europe it is not uncommon to find poets well-versed in chemistry, biology, engineering. Poetry is another extension of their creativity. In this country poetry is regarded as creative writing, as though creativity is expected to be absent from most other forms of writing. Perhaps this accounts for the tedium of most public documents and the obscurantism common in scientific and technical papers.

Until the early summer of 1996 Pace was an independent company whose directors were able to make quick decisions ensuring the minimum of delay between R&D, design, and production. But rapid expansion required a large amount of new capital. Unlike German banks, which offer good companies loans with a pay-back period of 20 years, British banks want their money back with interest in five or six years. That's why Pace's directors decided to float the company on the stock market.

Will the company look for a new base beyond Salts Mill? I do not think so, not this side of the Twentieth Century at any rate. Robert Fleming, pleased with the amicable relationship between landlord and tenant, sees no reason to move.

"We are a good tenant because we were early, we were sound. We are clean and we are the perfect partner, and that's ideal for Jonathan. We are seen as affluent; as a company we are profitable, the products we make are quality products. He doesn't do anything at Saltaire that's tacky, and we fit that very well. In terms of turnover it's a lot cheaper for us to be in Salts. Our business is dynamic: it can grow or shrink and there's no penalty for us if we do either," he said.

The mill's regenerative success has had a beneficial effect on the rest of Saltaire. In March 1994 Bradford Council surveyed tourism rates in villages throughout the country and discovered that Saltaire led the way. Numbers of visitors increased from 200,000 in 1990 to nearly 360,000 in 1993. During the summer months of 1994, Silver estimated that 10,000 people a week were visiting the mill, many of them curious to see David Hockney's dog drawings.

On the other side of the canal, the New Mill, a once derelict building (not owned by Silver) has been converted into offices for the Bradford Health Authority and quality private apartments. Silver has also invested more than £120,000 in fitting out 10,000 square feet of office and library space for the health authority, which has outgrown its premises in the New Mill.

In 1996 recognition rained down on Saltaire. No fewer than 15 organisations in the village, including the mill, received awards from the Civic Trust including the Boots Centre Vision Award, given for the most outstanding contribution to the improvement of a town or city centre. Saltaire beat off opposition from Edinburgh Opera House and London's new Waterloo Station. Among the improvements which so impressed the judges was Silver's conversion of Titus Salt's former coach house. He has spent many thousands of pounds transforming what was a stable into a four-bedroom house with many unique features, including a hand-carved staircase made entirely from cherry wood. The village itself, which has added a double-fronted emporium specialising in Victorian antiques to its shops, ambitiously wants an Italian-style piazza to make the most of the long days and balmy nights of summer, and a hotel.

The following year Saltaire hit the big time. The village beat 120 entrants from 20 European countries to win Europe's top award for conservation and restoration, the Europa Nostra IBI medal. Prince Henrik of Denmark presented the prize at a ceremony in Spain. To fully comprehend this and other of Saltaire's recent honours you must remember the state of the place before Jonathan Silver's arrival.

In 1987 Saltaire had a landscape and a renovated railway station. The village itself, however, was a stagnating backwater. Art and industry, commerce and culture, have changed that. More new building has taken place since 1993 than at any time since the 1870s. Restoration has followed transformation: that's how regeneration has worked in Saltaire.

The biggest single investment after Pace's £5 million factory, with stock and machinery valued at more than £50m, is attributable to what one might call Romancing the Phone. In November 1994 the Bradford-based company Filtronic Comtek plc, which makes signalling equipment for base stations for mobile telephones, announced a total investment of £4 million in a new four-storey building, containing a factory and offices, on a couple of scrubby acres to the east of Salts. Silver, who was paid £615,000 for the land, was like a cat with two tails for days afterwards.

"Where else in Bradford can you see a new factory being built?" he kept saying.

Better than at any other time in his business career he understood how Titus Salt felt when he saw Salts Mill rising from those 14 acres between the canal and the railway in the early 1850s

The Filtronic story is a good antidote to the V&A episode in that it offers an example of how the local authority and private business can work together in a way that benefits everyone.

If the green field site of about 4.5 acres had not been part of the purchase in 1987 Silver would not have bought the mill. It would have been a monolith with no land for car parking.

Two years of negotiations took place between Bradford Council's planning department and Salts Estates to agree a change of use for Salts, from heavy industry to retailing, leisure, offices and other uses. In return Salts Estates contributed £500,000 to the cost of a new road at the back of the mill (Silver had to borrow the money). Old Mill Road became Salts Mill Road, the first new thoroughfare to the mill since the days of Titus Salt.

Silver, aware that not all of the land nearby would be needed for parking, waited for what he hoped would be an ideal opportunity.

"I received a 'phone call from John Steel, at that time the Council's chief planning officer. He asked me if I knew of a company called Filtronic. I did, but I didn't know its boss - David Rhodes. John said Rhodes was looking to build a manufacturing base in Bradford, but was looking elsewhere. He said perhaps it was time for the green field site to be used. I then rang David Rhodes and we met within a few hours. He explained that he wanted a green field site and said he thought ours was going to be ideal. From that point to exchange of contracts was only two or three months".

"The concept of regeneration is advanced another stage by something of this magnitude because the cash allows for the continuity of the Salts Mill project."

In July 1995, Filtronic took a 20-year lease on two old prefabricated wool sheds between the mill and the new factory. Mark Vaux, Filtronic's operations director, described doing business with Jonathan Silver.

"He fights his corner very hard. He's very quick, and expects his support people to close things off very quickly. When we did the deal for the sheds I know his solicitors were working quite late into the evening on the deal. He doesn't like questions, he likes answers. I think most people would describe him as impatient. But they have a respect for what he's achieved; he's turned Saltaire around." Silver was recovering from an appendix operation when he heard that Filtronic had expressed interest in the two sheds.

"He wanted to know if we were serious," said Mark Vaux. "He was prepared to spend many thousands of pounds refurbishing the sheds up to the standard of a modern industrial unit, in return for a long lease and the normal rent for a normal industrial unit."

One Saturday morning Silver drove me to the site in his Mercedes convertible. The sheds were being stripped to their rusty skeleton. As he described the glass and stone bridge which would link the buildings to the new factory, he was at pains to emphasise the long-term significance of the deal for Salts Mill, as well as the village. The future, at least until the year 2015, had been secured.

Privately, he was pleased for personal reasons too. In the past he had been described as only a buying and selling wheeler-dealer; unfavourable comparisons were made with his friend and rival Sir Ernest Hall, as well as with Sir Titus Salt. Once again, Silver had demonstrated his capacity for confounding people, including me, who thought they knew him.

Silver says he insisted that Filtronic's factory be made of stone and have a slate roof, in keeping with mill and most of the buildings in the village. He is keen on authenticity. He persuaded Bradford Council not to tarmacadam part of Victoria Road outside the mill, and paid £5,000 towards the cost of restoring Titus Salt's original stone cobbles. The cheque was written on one of the cobbles, and was accepted by the bank.

Silver understands the attraction of the past and the part it can play in giving a place a realistic future. The completed factory looks perfectly in harmony with its neighbouring palace of art and culture. They are like two great stone ships moored peacefully by the side of the canal. Large new car parks for both have been provided. Silver was displeased with the landscaping of his car park and spent more than £10,000 on new plants, shrubs and trees to augment the setting.

There are two Silvers in the mill. After going his own way for many years following the demise of the Art and Furniture shop in Manchester, Robin has moved back into his brother's orbit. He and his wife Pat, who used to design clothes for Jonathan in the 1970s, have invested more than £100,000 in a store selling upmarket objects for the home.

Called The Home, it opened in March 1994, offering a wide range of colourful and eye-catching table, kitchen and glassware, pewter, clocks, lamps, utensils, ornamental pottery, vases, pots, pans, bedding, candles and gift stationery.

The wares are wittily arranged on tables, in cabinets, on shelves painted in bright primary colours, bringing together the elements of a busy kitchen, a nursery and an offbeat department store.

"Jonathan told us the mill was the ideal place," Robin said. "He showed us the space. It was covered with pigeon droppings, was dusty and grimy, hadn't been used for years. Pat said it would be ideal: it had huge windows with lots of light, and a high ceiling. Ideal for displaying things the way we wanted to display them.

"One of our potential suppliers came and looked at the place and thought we were absolutely mad. She wouldn't supply us.

"I have the naive and hopeful belief that if you have got the products people want to buy and serve people in the way they want to be served, they will come and find you wherever you are. It may take longer, but they will get through in the end."

Until 1994 I had no idea that Jonathan had a brother. When I was told I must confess that I needed a few minutes to assimilate the idea of another Jonathan Silver in the world. They are, however, quite different. Robin enjoys giving strangers the impression that he's simply an affable fellow who, unlike his brother, enjoys nothing better than passing the time of day with a chat. In fact Robin has a tenacious intelligence and can be a keen and provocative debater. He has a droll sense of humour and enjoys teasing you while disarmingly appearing not to do so. He gained a degree in anthropology from the London School of Economics and is nobody's fool. I like Robin, though his anecdotes can sometimes be infuriatingly protracted.

To reach The Home you have to go through Skopos Design's furniture store (they also have a fabric department in the basement), and the American-style Diner.

Like every other part of the mill now operational, a lot of money was spent on cleaning up, decorating and equipping the space for The Diner, which can seat more than 200 at its 45 tables. The Diner and the now-defunct Clothes Store cost Silver about £500,000 to fit out. The heating system for both cost in the region of £35,000, the burnished copper Expresso machine from Italy cost £6,500, the electrics £12,000, and the sound system about £15,000. David Hockney, who else, designed the menu. His laser-printed colour photographs of the area of Yorkshire around the eastern coastal town of Bridlington, where his mother retired to live, are all over the walls. The Diner is, in effect, a gallery too. Other colourful works by Hockney, and Silver's own hugely-enlarged photo-montages of Hockney and Alan Bennett, provide a feast for the eye while you wait for the soup, the salad, or the Cumberland sausage and mash. On bad days I have gone to the mill simply to cheer myself up with cappuccino and a cigar - and to admire the attractive young waitresses. The Diner has proved to be popular as well as commercially successful.

Robin Silver, an experienced retailer, says the mill's mixture of culture and commerce is not the norm in Britain.

"Most developers have a terribly rigid idea about the way they develop things. I think Jonathan has taken a lot of time and considers things very carefully, and that's why people outside regard this as a very bizarre mix. It's the juxtaposition of oddities that makes the place so interesting.

"People who come to visit Pace don't expect to see an electronics factory in this setting; they are confused and yet pleased. The picture in their mind is based on preconceptions, expectations - not reality. People like to go through an act of discovery; there's an element of adventure in all of us."

The adaptability of the mill was further demonstrated in the Spring of 1996. Tony Martinez's company - Chase Advanced Technologies moved from Salts to a custom built modern industrial Estate elsewhere in Bradford. Within a few weeks the 10,000 square foot space was stripped, cleaned and entirely redecorated to form an extension to both the Diner and Robin and Pat Silver's store. Jonathan typically spent hours literally driving the painters up the wall as he directed their work from all angles and distances. The Diner, which can now seat 370 people, may not be the biggest restaurant in the galaxy, but it surely must be the largest in Yorkshire.

In addition, Silver is spending £100,000 on stripping away some post-war shedding and creating a large outdoor piazza. This will restore that part of the mill's exterior to its original glory as well as add a new amenity which may be used as a space for theatrical events. This will be good news for companies like Northern Broadsides.

A couple of years ago, Silver asked Tony Harrison to write something special for the mill, a musical piece he suggested, with sets by David Hockney and maybe an appearance by Alan Bennett.

The exact format of the work is still fermenting in Harrison's busy brain. Whatever form the piece takes, it won't be the first work which the author of the comic drama, The Trackers of Oxyrhynchus, has written for Salts Mill. Poetry or Bust, you may remember, was the first. The story of how that particular work came about is worth telling.

One Sunday in June 1993, Harrison had gone to the Diner for what he thought was an uneventful lunch. I happened to be sitting at a neighbouring table interviewing Sir Marcus Fox MP about the latest Government crisis, and could see that Silver was in his Mission Impossible mode.

He had asked Harrison to write a play for Salts Mill, not only that but the work had to be ready for September - to coincide with the English premiere of Hockney's Very New Paintings. Alan South, who was still Jonathan's right hand man at the time, said Harrison was appalled.

Silver, never one to take no for an answer, conducted the protesting poet on a lightning tour of the mill and then invited him back to his chaotic office-cum-studio for a calming cup of coffee.

Amid the clutter on the desk, Harrison saw a ceramic plaque depicting the head of Dante. Being an avid collector of Dante images, he offered to buy this one (made by the pottery firm at Burmantofts). Silver said he could have it - in exchange for a play.

Jonathan Silver doesn't operate as most people do, Sir Ernest Hall told me. "The whole thing is a stage for him: he's there as principal actor and manager and he loves the drama of it, he loves to make mountains out of molehills. He doesn't do what people conventionally do; his thinking is absolutely radical and yet there's nothing of the humbug about him. He's absolutely honest in his personal relationships. There's no way he will take the line of least resistance."

Silver perhaps embodies the quality which Sir Ernest defined as the essence of success in his Arts Council lecture: the refusal to accept defeat.

14. SUNFLOWERS FOR HOPE AND JOY

"He's a loyal friend," Alan South once told me, "but never give him an opportunity to invent a quarrel. Jonathan has a very dramatic view of life. So if he finishes with people he invents some quarrel, a dispute, a cause, usually over obligations because he's very strong on obligation."

The dissolution of their working relationship is a case in point. Alan's contribution to the success of Salts Mill from 1987 to 1993 was enormous, as Silver willingly admits. So why did they part company?

"I knew something was wrong because when Alan came back from a trip to Los Angeles he worked for two weeks but never took his overcoat off. I think he found the constraint of working so very hard at Salts too much of a strain. Working for me cannot be easy because I am so demanding," Silver said.

"He worked incredibly hard for a number of years, doing everything you can imagine: working the box office for Poetry or Bust, supervising building work, looking after demanding tenants, demanding banks, demanding planning requirements, and a gallery that was increasingly demanding time in its operation and in hanging pictures.

"He liked the benefits of all this, which were clearly strong financial security and material well-being (he loves spending money), but on the other hand his mystic and spiritual heart found this not only paradoxical, but also he may have felt within himself that it wasn't honest for him, so he left. I told him he was stupid. He couldn't understand what I meant, probably still doesn't; but we do remain the best of friends.

"He's intelligent and brilliant. Alan is somebody whom I could completely trust, who would defend anything to the hilt - probably even coming to blows with someone even though he is a Quaker at heart." Alan will always be protectively fond of Silver.

"Jonathan's a great nagger, but only with people he loves (with others he doesn't bother). He can kill you with kindness, but he can also be an extremely irritating person to work for. He can be maddeningly particular."

Salts Mill is not a museum: things are changing all the time. There is always something new to be seen - the latest Hockney, a piece of Burmantofts, a new book.

The mill is not about standing still, but maintaining change. Robert Fleming said in five or six years' time it probably won't be what it is now; it will be what it has become. Salts Mill is all about realising its potential.

Sir Ernest Hall rightly pointed out that in his thinking Silver is absolutely radical.

The art of regeneration: Simon palmer's drawing of the 1853 Gallery in 1996.

Courtesy: Simon Palmer & Jonathan Silver

Alan South used another word, unconventional. Like his predecessor Sir Titus Salt, Silver is a visionary, if to be a visionary means seeing the obvious before anyone else.

For years the paintings of L.S. Lowry have been admired, particularly the "dream-scapes" of the industrial North, showing mills in cobbled streets, tucked away in the folds of hills and valleys. These paintings however, full of people either in close-up or in long-shot, are not in the least folksy. Lowry, as we know, also painted unpeopled sea-scapes. In his loneliness he also painted pictures of a more disturbing nature.

In 1995, Silver purchased a small painting called Portrait of a Young Man. Against a background of blue-green the subject, a cross between a pierrot and a corpse, stares fixedly out of the picture. After a while you get the eerie feeling that what you are looking at is a reflection. The painting is like a mirror in an M.R. James horror story, in which strange figures move out of the background and lean towards you.

Silver hung the painting in the 1853 Gallery, evidently much taken with his purchase.

I forgot about it until one day over lunch when Silver suddenly said: "Do you think a Lowry Gallery would be a good idea?"

Yes, I replied, knowing that whatever I said would make no difference; I could tell by the light in his eyes that he had already made up his mind. He was powerfully attracted to the idea of exhibiting Lowry's work in a location reflecting the industrial past and the present. Cobbles and chimneys, steep streets of terraced houses - Lowry's familiar iconography which can also be seen from the topmost windows of the mill.

Silver's first idea was to convert derelict space on the top floor into a Lowry Gallery where he would exhibit, for the first time in a mill, the painter's industrial dream-scapes. But in the course of his attempts to acquire a selection of Lowrys on loan he discovered the existence of a substantial number of paintings which had never been shown.

He told me that hardly any of them, and there were about 60 altogether, depicted the usual factories and matchstick men and women. These pictures, he said, were more personal and disquieting. I asked in what way. "Some are fetishistic; sexually charged is the best way I can describe them," he said, enjoying the air of mystery he was creating. "They are pictures of men, some in women's clothing, tied up."

He had spent weeks trying to obtain them. Renowned for being impatient, Silver can also be rather cat-like. A cat will crouch patiently for ages, tail twitching, waiting for the right moment to pounce. Jonathan too knows there is a right time and a wrong time to close a deal. So long as he feels reasonably sure of the outcome, he is content to wait for the moment of maximum opportunity.

But then a series of events persuaded him to change his mind. Jack Hook's wife had a heart attack, and then Silver was struck down by appendicitis. The operation was successful; but shortly afterwards he had an attack of jaundice and briefly turned bright yellow, like Gauguin's Christ. Nevertheless, he continued to go to work and make plans for the Lowry gallery. I saw him one Friday evening in early September and he talked about the pictures he hoped to acquire. During the course of our conversation I noticed that his stomach seemed to be distended and jokingly advised him to lay off the Diner's sticky toffee pudding.

The next thing I heard he had rushed off to London for some sort of medical examination. All he would say was that further surgery was necessary, something to do with his gall bladder. And then one overcast morning I went to the mill and was taken to one side by Jack Hook who told me that Jonathan had cancer.

Long ago Silver had told me: "If I fell under a bus tomorrow Salts Mill would carry on." That clouded morning I remember walking round the galleries trying to picture the place without him. I could not. Everything in it, the seemingly haphazard arrangement of things in the 1853 Gallery, bore his touch.

Everyone in the mill was trying to suppress their feelings. Silver was in the building and I guess no one wanted make things harder for him by being emotional. I went up to his office and pointlessly sat in the ante-room talking to Linda, his secretary. He quickly emerged from his study holding a blue canvas briefcase, a new one. He looked quite well. He smiled, shook hands, and said he was going. That was that. Silver dropped the Lowry idea. The acquisition of that painting of the young man, like a Voodoo doll, seemed to have brought a curse with it. The decision was a lucky one, for within months Salford secured millions of pounds from the National Lottery to build a brand new Lowry gallery in the artist's home town.

He was booked into the London Clinic to have a tumour removed from his pancreas. Pancreatic cancer, of course, can be fatal; it killed the television playwright Dennis Potter. Jonathan's wife and daughters were totally distraught. He says he felt so well he couldn't believe he wasn't going to have a good outcome.

He travelled to London with Maggie, Zoë and Davina on Saturday, September 24, 1995. Having a couple of hours to spare before the operation he took them shopping in Bond Street. Surgery was performed by Mr Christopher Russell. He had already explained the operation in detail to Jonathan and Maggie, telling them there was a 60-40 chance of a successful outcome. The alternative to surgery was one to three years more life. "Maggie and I decided we had an affinity with this fellow. He was just a delightful person," Silver told me later.

Early the following day I went down to Salts Mill. Jonathan's brother Robin had promised to tell me what had happened. The operation had lasted eight hours. For most of the time Maggie and the girls had held hands. Two hours after

One of David hockney's 'hot dogs'. A paper napkin design for the Diner.

Courtesy: David Hockney

it was all over they were allowed to have a look at Jonathan lying in intensive care. "They were rather astonished to see him wave at them," Robin said.

By the Tuesday the story, which had been kept quiet, was circulating Saltaire. I rang Silver's assistant Ray Shilling and told him that the story had to come out. Within 30 minutes my telephone rang. It was Silver, calling from his hospital bed to say that he had made a record recovery, was feeling very dynamic and expected to be home by Friday. This is what he said for the record:-

"Yes I have had a tumour which has now been removed. Yes they have taken away my duodenal and I no longer have a gall bladder. Tests have shown there is no growth left in my body anywhere. I feel a bit of a fraud really, but I have been seriously ill. This particular type of cancer is known as silent cancer. It started at the top of the pancreas and closed off the gall pipe, and that caused the jaundice. It was a highly complex piece of surgery seven hours in length. I came out of intensive care and eight hours later I started walking. I had a pipe in my nose, a pipe in my mouth, a pipe in my prick, and a drain. I was like something out of Dr Who or Frankenstein. I had a week of pain, but now I feel very wonderful and happy. I have not been ordered to do anything, I shall just let my body guide me. I was extremely healthy prior to the operation. I am not the sort of person to lie down and say, Oh my God I've had cancer, my life is changing! But it would be naive of me to say certain things won't change. The way I view life might have a little more maturity. On the other hand I might become more frivolous than ever. I don't think my recuperation period is going to be as long as people thought. I'm on the phone to the mill every day as it is."

He later said the whole experience had intensified the closeness between himself, his wife and their daughters. "I never thought I was going to die, so I just concentrated on getting it done and getting better. Maggie was there all the time, holding my hand. Zoë and Davina were there. The whole place was like a flower shop. I got hundreds of cards. I did take some of my own pictures to the hospital with me - a Cezanne print which had cost me £10."

He also received a get well painting from David Hockney called Sunflowers for Jonathan. A smaller painting called Sunflowers for Hope and Joy, was made available as a postcard. Hockney flew to Yorkshire as soon as he heard about the cancer. For a time there had been talk of flying Jonathan to Philadelphia for the operation. Hockney's 94-year-old mother Laura had sent Jonathan a little drawing of flowers which she had done for him. The threat to yet another of his friends was to galvanise Hockney, who was then staying with his mother in Bridlington. He set about a series of intensely painted portraits.

Before entering hospital, Silver had contacted the comedienne and comic actress Victoria Wood. He wanted her to perform in concert at Salts Mill later in the year, in aid of Bradford's Cancer Support Centre. Then he wrote telling her that he had cancer himself. She agreed to perform on Sunday, March 3, 1996. Silver put 250 tickets on sale at £100 a time. They were sold within five days.

In the months before the big night Silver had plenty to occupy him. He had returned to Salts the day after leaving hospital, eager to see for himself the progress of the Filtronic factory and how well the public had received the publication of Saltaire: a Picture Storybook - a book of paintings on the theme of Saltaire by Simon Palmer. The proofs of the richly-coloured book had been sent down to the London Clinic, which is where both David Hockney and Alan Bennett saw them. They approved. Hockney in particular enjoyed them.

Palmer, born in Doncaster in 1956, is primarily a landscape artist. His wife, Tink, had sent postcards of her husband's work to Silver who thought they were fabulous. He commissioned the artist to paint a picture of Saltaire. The result was an extremely large watercolour called Titus Salt and the Bible Women. The very first time Silver showed it to me I was bowled over. Its pale brassy golds, shadowy greens and purple-greys gave it the feel of one of those old colour plates that illustrate Bible stories. But in

Singing Salts Mill's praises in the rain. Prince Charles enthuses to Jonathan Silver as he arrives at Salts in October 1996 for a long and significant visit.   *Photo: Salts Estates*

the exaggerated size of Salt's gold fob watch there was a touch of Alice in Wonderland about it too. Palmer produced another 12 watercolours. Silver had them framed and hung them round the walls of his office. The best of them capture and evoke the timelessness of Saltaire and deserve a wider audience.

I encouraged Silver to put the pictures in his new gallery on the fourth floor, but he had other plans in mind. The paintings which Hockney had been painting with ferocious concentration at Bridlington were to dominate the wonderful new space above the Diner which was opened on the night of Victoria Wood's charity cabaret. Silver was in his element: Victoria Wood, 250 guests, the promise of £37,000 raised for charity, and ten new paintings by David Hockney - all on the one night. Where else in England could such an event happen?

Fortunately, I had already seen the paintings before that night, as had two friends of mine. What struck them was the serenity with which Hockney had depicted his mother, lying in bed. It was not the nearness of death they found in the pictures, as one newspaper critic did, but tenderness. The portrait of Jonathan is the most intensely painted of all. His face and head are sharply modelled with cutting flicks of paint. The eyebrows, eyes, nose and mouth depict melancholy and a gaunt humility. This is a man contemplating the loss of everything he loves. The title of the painting could be: Life's Only Certainty is Uncertainty. This revealing portrait also shows the change in Silver since 1987, when I first met him. The jet black hair is now longer, streaked with argent and grey. The snappy dresser in tight blue jeans and collarless shirts now wears an avuncular blue cardigan and baggy Chaplinesque trousers. His physical contours are less sharply defined. But this bagginess denotes kindliness, I think, not slackness or carelessness. Though Silver's eyes are ringed by darker bags from the pain he occasionally suffers as a result of such extensive surgery, his mind remains as bright as a newly-minted coin.

Looking at the paintings I recalled that interview with Hockney on the night of the Alan Bennett reading. What he said about Van Gogh and the necessity of love came back to me. Van Gogh's hand was on Hockney's shoulder when he painted those pictures. But they remain distinctly Hockney's; there is no suggestion of plagiarism and certainly not pastiche. These pictures are an emphatic rebuttal of those critics who judge Hockney by his occasional self-indulgence - all those paintings of his dogs, for example.

Critics are suspicious of Hockney's eclecticism. They cannot easily define or even summarise such wide-ranging work and so Hockney is regarded as a brilliantly-coloured gadfly. Or else he remains stuck in a time-warp, the enfant terrible of the 1960s, despite the fact that he has moved on and keeps moving on. Bob Dylan, whose enormous and varied musical output similarly defies definition, once said that he tried to keep one step ahead of himself. "That's my foolish mission," he added. I think Hockney is trying to stay one step ahead of himself.

In October 1996 another eclectic arrived at Salts Mill. Prince Charles alighted from the royal train at Saltaire, greeted the awaiting crowd with smiles and handshakes, and then walked across the road to the mill. He spent more than two hours viewing the galleries, looking round the businesses, and taking part in two meetings. One of them was held in the Sir Titus Salt's board room, the other took place in Salt's former stable which Silver has converted into a splendid family home.

The board room meeting was a seminar for members of the Prince's Regeneration Through Heritage initiative and representatives of three pilot projects in Lancashire and Yorkshire. This initiative was set up by the Business in the Community organisation at the Prince's request. The heir to the throne is the organisation's president. The aim of Regeneration Through Heritage is to bring together private sector resources and local people to conserve fine old industrial buildings and create new opportunities for jobs, training, and social gatherings. Salts Mill, of course, was the ideal location. It represented everything the Prince had envisioned, and he was genuinely thrilled and impressed by what he saw. Afterwards Silver remarked to me upon the Prince's complete lack of self-importance, and upon his evident commitment to the causes he espoused.

In a speech some time after his visit to Saltaire the Prince declared: "I was delighted to see what Jonathan Silver has achieved at Salts Mill. I was particularly struck by the quality of what he has done and the way he has put renovated space to such good use. It was wonderful to see a hi-tech business located within a 19th Century mill."

The royal seal of approval was personally pleasing to me. I had long felt that Silver had not received the recognition which his astonishing achievements deserved. The honorary Fellowship bestowed on him by Bradford & Ilkley Community College in December 1996, in recognition of his contribution to the Arts, was long overdue.

Salts Mill is not an industrial museum, nor a kind of cultural theme park for the offspring of people who wear rumpled linen jackets. It embodies the key difference between the concepts of restoration and regeneration. Restoration preserves whereas regeneration transforms. Salts Mill is simply the triumphant physical manifestation of the mind and imagination of two men: Salt and Silver. On certain days this potent amalgam can be overpowering.

I experienced this one October afternoon in 1994, a Tuesday afternoon of uplifting autumnal beauty, a golden day in fact.

I had come from lunching with Paul Hockney in Shipley and had walked down to the mill, its pale gold stone glowing in the warmth of the sun. You have to be in love to taste the bitter-sweet nuances of such a day. And I was in love.

In this emotionally lyrical state, I entered the 1853 Gallery. Late afternoon light was blazing through most of the 44 tall windows. The silver-painted iron columns gleamed and the ceiling's terra-cotta coloured brick arches radiated both coolness and warmth, like the interior of a great cathedral. The colours of the pictures, the scent of the lilies, the opera pouring out of the black Bose speakers, all this exalted what I felt.

Jonathan, I was told, was not in the best of moods, being a bit short-staffed that day. He was busy in the Diner, but waved a greeting. Eventually he came over and showed me the new menu he had just finished. Then he took me on a whirlwind tour of Pace's new warehouse in a part of the mill that had not been operational since World War II. The walls had been sandblasted and painted. The floor was stacked with electrical components manufactured in the mill.

I was happy to see all this, and something of my mood was obviously rubbing off, for he insisted on fetching a torch to give me a conducted tour of the huge subterranean space running for perhaps 230 yards along the entire length of the building on the canal side, a space I had never seen before.

We explored this nether region like a couple of characters in Orpheus in the Underworld, except that neither of us burst into song. Under the floor was Titus Salt's reservoir, a tank capable of holding several hundred thousand gallons of water. Sixteen feet above was the ceiling, and in between a mezzanine floor which, Jonathan gleefully explained, he intended to rip out. Eagerly he showed me a part of this vast space which had already been renovated. This was what the rest of it would look like. The mezzanine had been taken out and the vaulted brickwork of the ceiling exposed and cleaned. It was like being in the catacomb below an Italian cathedral.

"Imagine frosted glass in the windows," he said.

These windows, each about 15 feet or more in height, arched the entire length of the canal wall. Through them glinted sunlit water and the cleaned stonework of the New Mill. One April evening, about 18 months later, through a window in the New Mill I gazed at other side of this wall, so solid, so peaceful, suffused with the mineral light of timeless generations. The green canal moved without noise, almost the same colour as the mill's window frames and doors. I thought of Blake's line about Christ in ancient time walking on England's hills of green. I felt moved as I had been when I heard John Tavener's The Protecting Veil and the last swelling chords of Gotterdammerung - symbolising both the end and the beginning of the world.

"Sometimes I imagine Titus Salt himself as the poet of his age," says Carl Dawson in his book Living Backwards: A Transatlantic Memoir. Dawson, a professor of literature in the United States, had spent his childhood in Saltaire. "A visionary like the Brontës or Wordsworth, he was private and retiring, driven to make what he knew best how to make. Wordsworth spoke of silent poets who lived a kind of poetry. He would not have included Salt among the gifted few, yet Salt had a visionary power. Without sorting the wool (like his employee, Joseph Wright) or weaving the cloth, Salt did in a sense spin the yarn, write his own story in iron and stone, driving others as he drove himself with ruthless creative energy. I can in my invented past create Salt and his mill as if I remembered them, as if to spin the yarn myself." So too can I.

Either Jonathan did not know or did not feel inclined to disclose his plans for this dark and dusty space. A great deal of money would be needed, about £3 million he thought. The point was, he was showing me the future. Having so much space available would allow him to maintain change, to let the mill become whatever it was going to become.

"I'm not interested in the past, as you know," he said, as we emerged from the twilight into the early evening sunshine. "Now I'm going in there," he added, pointing to the 1853 Gallery, filled with sunlight and the sound of grand pianos, "and anything could happen. That's the way I like it."

ACKNOWLEDGEMENTS

BOOKS

The Age of Optimism (Milestones of History), Newsweek Books,
   Weidenfeld and Nicholson, 1974.
The Birth of Europe, by Michael Andrews, BBC Books 1991.
The Western Intellectual Tradition, by Jacob Bronowski and Bruce Mazlish,
   Hutchinson & Co. Ltd., 1960.
Civilisation, by Kenneth Clark. Pelican Books 1982.
Ruskin and Bradford: An Experiment in Victorian Cultural History, by
   Malcolm Hardman, Manchester University Press 1986.
The Great Paternalist: Titus Salt and the Growth of Nineteenth Century Bradford, by
   JackReynolds.
Maurice Temple Smith, in association with the University of Bradford. 1983.
Yorkshire Textile Mills 1770-1930: Commission on the
   Historical Monuments of England (West Yorkshire Archaeology Service),
   by Colum Giles and Ian H Goodall, HMSO 1992.
Yorkshire Past and Present Vol. 1, published by William Mackenzie round about 1870.
Bradford, by Joseph Fieldhouse, revised edition, Watmoughs Ltd and Bradford
   Libraries 1978.
Titus Salt and Saltaire: Industry and Virtue, by John Styles, second edition, Salts
   Estates Ltd 1994.
The Bradford Antiquary 1987.
Salts Mill & Museum: A Short History and Guide by Donald Hanson,
   (research by J. Stanley King).
Saltaire and its Founder, by Abraham Holyroyd, 1873.
Sir Titus Salt: His Life and Its Lessons, by Robert Balgarnie, 1877.
Titus of Salts, edited by Roger Suddards, 1976.
Saltaire, an introduction to the village of Sir Titus Salt, by Jack Reynolds. Published by
   Bradford Art Galleries & Museums, 1976.
Living Backwards: A Transatlantic Memoir, by Carl Dawson, University Press of
   Virginia, 1995.

MAGAZINES AND NEWSPAPERS

The Bradford Observer: December 13th 1849.
The Practical Magazine Vol. 3, 1874.
Harpers New Monthly Magazine, undated but before 1876.
The Engineer, January 5th 1877.
The Bradford Observer: December 30th 1876 and January 6th 1877.
The Telegraph & Argus: November 10th 1987 (Jonathan Silver profile).
The Telegraph & Argus: July 26th 1988 (Sir Ernest Hall profile).

The Telegraph & Argus: October 31st 1995 (Pace's recruitment problem).
The Telegraph & Argus: November 3rd 1995 (Bradford's hi-tech future).
The Telegraph & Argus: October 4th 1995 (Jonathan Silver interview after operation).
The Telegraph & Argus: December 13th 1995 (Simon Palmer profile).
The Independent: July 27th 1994 (Jonathan Glancey article).
The Independent on Sunday: October 2nd 1994 (John Arlidge article).

RESEARCH PAPERS

David Dale: Founder and Creator of New Lanark, by David J McLaren.
Robert Owen as a Political Theorist, by Lyman Tower Sargent.
Department of Political Sciences, University of Missouri, Presented to the first meeting
   of the International Communal Studies Association, New Lanark, Scotland, July 1988.
Utopian Thought and Communal Experience, by Auraham Yassour, University of
   Haifa, presented July 1988.

Thanks are due to the Telegraph & Argus, Bradford, for some of the photographs, and to staff of Bradford Central Library who helped me at the outset of my research back in July, 1994. Bob Duckett took an interest in the project in 1996 following the generous intercession of my friend and former colleague Alan Whitaker, and brought it to publication. Thanks also to everyone who agreed to be interviewed: Paul Hockney, David Hockney, Jonathan Silver, Robin Silver, Sydney and Irene Silver, Alan South, Robert Fleming, Jack Hook, Sir Ernest Hall, Maurice Miller, Ronnie Farley, Colin Clavering, Clive Woods, Alan Lewis, John Collins, Stanley J. King, Peter Booth, and Mark Vaux. Thanks especially to Ray, for a spell this book's de facto editor, who spent many hours scrutinising the text and making suggestions. Thanks also to my late friend and fatherly encourager Roger Suddards CBE. He read the sixth version of the book, offered many perceptive suggestions, some of which I adopted, and resolutely believed in it.